*The* LIONS
*and*
*the* LAMBS

# The Lions and the Lambs

by THOMAS FENSCH

Professional billiards—pool hustling—is a sport that has fascinated men for years. Pool is an old, old game. In *Antony and Cleopatra*, William Shakespeare gave *Cleopatra* the line, "Come, let's to billiards." Billiards was a favorite sport during Shakespeare's time. Mary Queen of Scots is known to have played the game. Later, Lord Byron wrote: "You'll never guess, I'll bet you millions and millions. It all sprang from a harmless game of billiards."

Today pool hustlers are thought to be furtive, stereotyped characters, as popularized by Twentieth-Century Fox's film *The Hustler,* starring Jackie Gleason and Paul Newman. There are perhaps more misconceptions about billiards than any other sport. Now, for the first time, *The Lions and the Lambs* cuts through the myths and presents the sport and its participants as they really are. It should be emphasized that until this compilation there has been no decent book about billiards, and particularly no book-length treatment that separates the facts of billiards (especially as a business—hustling) from the legends surrounding this most masculine of sports.

A *Lion*, in the language of the players, means a gambler or hustler, one who can win when there is money on the table, a player with heart, or courage, but not necessarily a tournament winner. Some lions discussed in this book are Ronnie Allen, Don Willis, U. J. Puckett, and William "Cornbread Red" Burge.

*Lambs* are fun players who play to win tournaments but not necessarily money, such as Joe "The Meatman" Balsis; Stanley Morycz; Mary Canelos; Gail Allums, perhaps the best collegiate player of recent years; Sheila Bohm; and Robert Froeschle, a leading tournament official.

Mr. Fensch, a pool player himself when he has time, writes about the people who play billiards day after day, month after month. Each chapter is a comprehensive profile of the player—his (or her) interests, attitudes towards the game, and comments on other players—something that has never been done before in this area. The author has included many photographs (most of which he has taken himself) of each player to supplement his informative text. He also provides a Lexicon of Pool for the reader's reference and a Chart of Standings that includes the name of the player, home town, earnings for each game—nine-ball, 14.1, and one-pocket—and total earnings.

*The Lions and the Lambs* is factual. It is accurate. It will be read by the Lions and the Lambs themselves, and will be valued as well by all interested spectators and avid participants.

---

This is a reprint of the original 1970 edition.

*Also by Thomas Fensch...*

*Steinbeck and Covici: The Story of a Friendship*
*Conversations with John Steinbeck*
*The FBI Files on Steinbeck*
*Essential Elements of Steinbeck*
*Steinbeck's bitter fruit:*
    *from The Grapes of Wrath to Occupy Wall Street*
*The Man Who Was Dr. Seuss: The Life and Work*
    *of Theodor Geisel*
*Of Sneetches and Whos and the Good Dr. Seuss:*
    *Essays on the Life and Work of Theodor Geisel*
*The Man Who Was Walter Mitty:*
    *The Life and Work of James Thurber*
*Conversations with James Thurber*
*The Man Who Changed His Skin:*
    *The Life and Work of John Howard Griffin*
*Behind Islands in the Stream:*
    *Hemingway, Cuba, the FBI and the crook factory*
*Oskar Schindler and His List:*
    *The Man, the Book, the Film, the Holocaust and*
    *Its Survivors*
*Foreshadowing Trump:*
    *Trump Characters, Ethics, Morality and Fascism in Classic Literature*
*Timeless (Pen) Names:*
    *The Life and Work of Charles Lutwidge Dodgson,*
    *Samuel Langhorne Clemens, Eric Blair and Theodor Geisel*
*The Kennedy-Khrushchev Letters*
*Orwell in America*

... and others ...

# The LIONS and the LAMBS

*Pool Players and the Game Today*

by Thomas Fensch

**New Century Books**

Copyright © 1970, 2020 by Thomas Fensch

All rights reserved. No part of this book may be reproduced or utilized in any form or by any means, electronic or mechanical, including photocopying or recording, or by any other information storage or retrieval system, without written permission from the publisher.

New Century Books 8821 Rockdale Rd.
N. Chesterfield, Va, 23236-2150
newcentbks@gmail.com

ISBN: 978-1-7333293-9-2 (paperback)

Second edition published in 2020
First published in 1970
Library of Contress Catalogue Card Number: 74-88251

Printed and bound in the USA

---

Photos by the author unless otherwise noted.

Extract in Chapter 18 from pp. 36-37
THE HUSTLER by Walter Tevis.
Copyright © 1959 by Walter Tevis.
By permission of Harper & Row, Publishers.

*To my parents
and
to Richard Gehman*

# *Contents*

| | |
|---|---|
| *Introduction*—The World of Pool | 9 |

### PART I
### The Lions — 17

1. Ronnie Allen—No Dark Horse Now — 19
2. Tom Kollins—the Dee Jay — 28
3. Don Willis—The Unknown Lion — 35
4. U. J. Puckett—Mr. One-Pocket — 43
5. Sonny Springer—The Southern Gentleman — 48
6. William Burge—Cornbread Red — 53
7. Pete Margo—The Youngest Lion — 58
8. Hustling in Johnston City — 66

### PART II
### The Lambs — 83

9. Joe Balsis—The Next Mosconi — 85
10. Ardell LaSieur—Spirit of St. Louis — 95
11. Stanley Morycz—King of Coney Island — 99
12. Sheila Bohm—Impatient for Stardom — 107
13. Jimmy Cattrano, Jr.—The Legacy of Hoppe — 114
14. Verne Peterson—They Call Him the "Slide Rule." — 123
15. Mary Canelos—Co-ed with a Hot Stick — 131
16. Gail Allums—Iowa's Number One Double Threat — 139
17. Robert Froeschle—Man in the Middle — 145
18. The Hustler—The Renaissance of Pool — 152

*Glossary*—An Abridged Lexicon of the Game — 158
*Appendix*—Who Earns How Much — 163

"A Chicago Pool-Room on Sunday" from a magazine of the 1890s. (Courtesy Billiard Archives)

# Introduction – The World of Pool

"The very rich," F. Scott Fitzgerald once said, "are different from you and me." "Yes," Ernest Hemingway replied, "they have more money." Pool hustlers *are* different from you and me too, but they don't necessarily have more money. What they do have is a different view of the world—especially the world of money and how to make it.

Pool is an old, old game. In *Anthony and Cleopatra*, William Shakespeare gave Cleopatra the line, "Come, let's to billiards." Billiards was a favorite sport during Shakespeare's time. Mary Queen of Scots is known to have played the game. Later, Lord Byron wrote: "You'll never guess, I'll bet you millions and millions. It all sprang from a harmless game of billiards."

In America the game was introduced by the Spaniards, who brought it to St. Augustine, Florida in 1565. The game grew to be very popular before the Civil War and in April 1859, championship was played between Michael Phelan of New York and John Secreiter of Detroit for $15,000—an almost unheard-of figure during those times.

Later, in this country, billiards as a game declined in popularity for a variety of reasons. It was known to be a part of the *Police Gazette* way of life—sordid, dirty, and cheap—and it was scorned by the decent citizens of the country. Vaudeville, radio, and other entertainment means also helped kill it too. For many years, billiards was not thought to be a gentleman's game.

But curiously, the depression helped return the game

to its former prominence. Thousands of men, out of work and almost penniless, returned to the pool halls to try and make some money on the game. Several of the current experts at the green tables, men like Don Willis, began to play during the 1930s, when there were few other areas open to them, to make some money. Most quit the game when times got better and money was freer, but some, like Willis, continued bending over the tables in smoke-filled halls, hustling for their living.

W. C. Fields, who made the famous statement, "never give a sucker an even break," was talking about the break shot, the first shot in a game of pool. The term later spread to other areas of life as well, but Fields knew what he was talking about. He was an expert at the game, a trick shot artist who showed his stuff on trick tables, with a bent cue, in vaudeville, before he began the films that made him famous.

Now in the 1970s there are fewer and fewer places to gamble on the game. The billiard industry would like to convince everyone that billiards is a "family sport" that the wife and kiddies can play. Tables are now being made with covers of red, pink, blue, and tan instead of the traditional green, and "family billiard parlors" are springing up in shopping centers, with women's leagues, and with attached restaurants.

There are few public rooms in which gambling is allowed. So the billiards hustler, the man who makes his living at the game, must travel from room to room, from city to city, constantly on the go, or risk revealing his identity and ability and thereby losing his source of livelihood.

Or they can gather at tournaments like the Johnston City tournament or the Stardust in Las Vegas and play each other.

Most pool hustlers have nicknames, due to the spirit of kinship and pride that the pros have for the game.

Some nicknames are indicative of physical characteristics—"Boston Shorty," "Handsome Danny" Jones, who looks like actor James Garner, and V. J. "Ugly" Prickett.

Others result from either ancedotes or part-time, non-billiard occupations. William "Weenie Beenie" Staton has two hot-dog stands by that name near Washington D.C., and Eddy "The Knoxville Bear" got his nickname from U. J. Puckett, as noted in the chapter on Puckett.

Billiards hustling is a dying art financially. The few tournaments that the hustlers can play in are not financially as rewarding as professional golf, for instance. A glance at the Standings list at the end of this book will reveal that the total prize money for the world of billiards for one year wouldn't equal a major P.G.A. golf tournament, a tournament that Arnold Palmer or Gary Player could win in a few days.

But occasionally the sky is the limit in hustling, depending on location and backers. Some hustlers have played as high as $2,000 a game, and with that kind of money the game is tense. Ronnie Allen once played with that kind of action on the line and when he did, he had five FBI agents and several Las Vegas bookies watching every shot. The FBI men were there to see that everyone had federal gambling stamps and the bookies were there to watch their money.

Ronnie, who is called "Fast Eddie" after the Paul Newman role in *The Hustler*, took home $40,000.

Few report their true earnings on their income tax. To do so would invite a visit from the Internal Revenue Service, because it would reveal the source of their income—gambling. Consequently, most report a fraction of their earnings or they list sidelines. They list such saccharine occupations as part owner of a billiards hall or something similar.

Unlike professional football players, who can't stand the pounding, or professional baseball players, whose legs go bad, the eyes of a pool player are usually the first to go. "They don't have to get very bad until you can't see the edge of the ball—it gets fuzzy. Then you might as well quit—it doesn't take but a fraction of an inch to miss a shot," one hustler said.

Or sometimes a player can't stand the grinding, debilitating, hour-after-hour pace of the game. Some older players just don't have the stamina they had when they were younger, and a player must depend on stamina to get him through marathon games.

This book is an attempt to explain the world of pool as it exists today. Pool players are human too, and when they talk about the game and themselves and each other, they complain just like plumbers or bricklayers or school teachers complain about their professions. There isn't enough money in it. The work is hard. It is lonely. It is too tough. It is not an easy way to raise a family. It is dying.

But it *is* unique and the players in the game today love it. They might not say so, but they do. Pool players —money players—take an intense pride in their craft. For tournaments they dress well, use expensive cues, and wear diamond rings. They play hard and win enough to live on, some better than others.

It should be understood that throughout this book, when players talk about "billiards" they generally refer to the variations of *pocket* billiards—straight pool, nine-ball or one-pocket. Rarely do they mean three-cushion billiards, which is not a very popular game and certainly not a hustlers' game. When three-cushion is mentioned, it is mentioned by name.

There are certainly other players that could have been mentioned in this book. Luther "Wimpy" Lassiter, who is currently one of the best tournament players and was one of the best hustlers in the game, could have been mentioned. Irving Crane, who sells Cadillacs on the side in Rochester, New York, might also have deserved a chapter. Eddy Taylor, the best bank-pool player in the country is only pictured beside U. J. Puckett. Eddy Kelly might have been given space, as well as Danny Jones, Willie Mosconi, Boston Shorty, Dallas West, Cisero Murphy, or several others. I do not pretend that this book is a comprehensive anthology of the game and its players. I do, however, suggest that the players in this book are a representative sample of those in the game today, from top money winners like Joe Balsis and Ronnie Allen, to those for whom pool is an interesting avocation, like Gail Allums, Mary Canelos, and Bob Froeschle.

I would also hope that this book separates the myth of the world of pool as seen in *The Hustler* from the actual world of pool, without all the fables and anecdotes. Pool is a way of life and there will always be stories told about it—some true and some not-so-true. For many, the only information they have about the game are the not-so-true stories told second hand, passed along from player to player in small-town pool halls. The fables sometimes make the world of pool seem larger than life, more glamorous, more exciting, more lucrative. Unfortunately it is not always what it seems.

This is the way it actually is.

*The* LIONS
*and*
*the* LAMBS

*Part I*

# THE LIONS

... in pool, a gambler or hustler, who can win when there is money on the table—his or a backer's. A player with "heart" or courage, but not necessarily a tournament winner.

# 1
## *Ronnie Allen – No Dark Horse Now*

"In professional golf, you can be a professional at 25. You're ready to retire from the game at 35. In professional football, you're ready to retire at 35. Almost all other sports—professional sports—when you're 35, you've had it. But it takes a pool player 15 years to gain the right kind of experience for the game."

But Ronnie Allen, at 29, contradicts his own argument. He is a consistent winner after only a few years at the game. He makes impressive showings in the tournaments he enters.

"I won $15,000 in 1966," he says, "placing first in two tournaments. I won the Long Beach, California Western Open and then the Las Vegas Stardust Open. I was second in three tournaments—the Johnston City tournaments and a couple of others, $15,000."

"It's pretty tough. Only the top four or five players in the game can make a living from it. From tournament winnings. There were five big tournaments in 1966 and three in 1967. Prize money was $63,000. Divide that by forty or so regulars in the tournaments, then take our expenses and travel and we'd all go broke."

Going broke is no longer a concern for him. He wins consistently.

"I worked for nine years at billiards and did other things on the side. Selling, for instance. I was in business

Ronnie Allen, only pool player to finance a new car as a "professional billiard player."

and out again. I was subscription manager for the *Saturday Evening Post*, for example. I did things like that for a living. Finally I quit altogether and began playing pool all the time. I'm improving all the time now.

"After Johnston City (in October and November of

1968), I'll go the Las Vegas tournament. The Jansco brothers—George and Paulie—have a nine-ball tournament in Los Angeles that I'll make and I'm working on promoting a tournament in Tucson, Arizona." *

Allen has definite ideas about how pool tournaments should be organized. He doesn't like the way most of them are run—from a player's point of view and from a business standpoint.

"For one thing, most of them are too long. It's too much to expect a man to play night and day for 30 days just to win a tournament. I'd make most tournaments a week long or a week and one-half at the most. They should be single elimination too. That way, they are interesting, exciting and easy to understand. If a player loses, he's out automatically. The spectators could tell who is ahead. There should be more profit for the winner. It's ridiculous for the winner of a major pool tournament to get $3,000 for 30 days of solid work.

"I'm usually so tired after the Jansco's Johnston City tournament that I go home and sleep for 30 days, just to catch up.

"There would be another advantage to having tournaments that last only one week. There is plenty of time to travel back and forth and still be able to spend time at home most of the month. The tournaments are so long now and most of them are boring when you aren't playing—all you have to do is drink and gamble.

"But for the tournaments that are played now—I'll take the Las Vegas tournament over any other—it's head over heels above the rest, as far as prize money to the winner and playing conditions are concerned.

"Billiard players need someone like Mark McCormack —the attorney who represents professional golfers like Gary Player and Jack Nicklaus. Pool players have got to

---

* Allen's grandiose Arizona tournament never happened.

get the tournaments straightened out and get better promotion and better playing conditions."

No matter how long Allen talks about pool, he eventually turns to professional golf.

"If I had the time, there's nothing better I'd like to do than play professional golf on the P.G.A. tour. But I'm not good enough for it. I have a ten handicap—that's an average score of 80–81. I'm satisfied with my golf game but I don't have time for pool and golf. In a sense they are similar games. Both are very hard to learn to play.

"Golfers and pool players have a lot in common physically, I think. I would like to talk with Arnold Palmer and Jack Nicklaus to see if they play well under the same kind of circumstances. I play best when I've slept well, after I've eaten, and when I'm keyed up. I hear that crowd and know the prize money and the side bets are there and I start shaking and tingling all over. After a few minutes I settle down, but the adrenaline keeps pumping and I keep going, all keyed up.

"I guess my best game is one-pocket. But I think I am unusual in that I play every game pretty well. I can play one-pocket one-handed to Wimpy Lassiter's two-hands. I never played much straight pool. That's an eastern game and my home was originally Oklahoma City. I'd like to tar and feather the guy who first invented straight pool. But I'm getting better at it.

"I recently improved my game over 20 percent. I watched Dallas West. He has the best break of anyone in the game. I watched him and watched him and watched him. I was just putting my arm in it . . ." Allen demonstrates, holding an imaginery stick, ". . . West throws his whole body behind the break, just like a golfer . . ." He shoots through a break-shot, with terrific force, scattering an invisible rack of balls. "I've been shooting like that lately and the break has improved for me.

Ronnie Allen.

"I don't think that there is a limit on perfection in billiards like there is in other sports. You can bowl a 300 game and that's it—you can't bowl 301. But there is no limit like that in pool. You should be able to just keep getting better and better.

"There's a whole argument about what kind of billiards is tougher, tournament play or "back-room play," where there is money riding on the game. Minnesota Fats claims that tournament play is nice and all, but there is no point to it unless there is some money on the table. I don't think that way at all.

"In the tournaments you start shooting and it's tough, just as tough or perhaps tougher than playing for cash. Do you know about that adrenalin too? Sure tournament play is tough.

"I have known guys like Fats who think that hustling is enough because your money or other people's money—O.P.M.—is riding on your shots. To some guys the idea of money on them makes them sick—actually physically sick.

"But as far as I'm concerned, the tournaments are tougher. I'd have to say one thing though, now that I've won some tournaments. No one wants to talk to me anymore, much less put some money on the table. That's the effect winning some tournaments has. You can't get up a good game, between tournaments.

"I don't know whether you can make much hustling or not. In Nevada, where it is legal you can make a little, but not enough to count on.

"I'm a professional pool player. Even my bank recognizes that. I have excellent credit and my car loan states 'professional pool player.' " He laughs, "I have this friend at the bank . . .

"I think that I am the only professional who is able to finance anything on the strength of his play. I never have been behind on the payments either. I've had this arrangement with the bank for the last five or six years.

"Yes, the tournaments are the thing. When I get keyed up and start shooting, I get faster and faster. Ed Butera (who is called "Machine Gun" Butera) is faster than I am, though. I've had people come out of the crowd at tournaments—people who don't know anything about the game and they'll tell me you're playing too fast, slow down. I'll tell you a secret, if I slowed down, I couldn't make a ball. I'd fall apart.

"There is such a thing as being too slow. Cisero Murphy drives me crazy. He'll examine for 30 minutes—at least—a ball that is hanging on the lip of the pocket. I couldn't do that. Give me a quicker game. That slow game just isn't my style.

"I guess I live like that too. Sixteen-hour days are too short for everything. I've been working all day every day for the last four months. I stayed up nearly three days and three nights at Johnston City. But when I get a chance, I'll catch up on my sleep and rest.

"People criticize pool because tournament play means that guys have to be away from home for weeks at a time. They forget that when we're home, we're home all the time. My wife Fay doesn't like me to be away, but I'm not away from home all that much. We live in Burbank, California, and it's nice—a nice neighborhood to live. Peaceful. A nice place to raise a family. We have two children, Reyna, six, and Tracey, seven. It's funny; last year I promised the kids that I'd win at Johnston City. When I placed second, I had to un-promise 'em. But I just explained what happened and it was OK with them.

"Billiards players are a breed of their own. They just don't like to be tied down with a lunch pail every day. Just like other professionals. Professional golfers, for instance. You play if you feel like it and if you don't you don't have to. That's reason enough for me to play the game.

"People used to call me 'Junior,' because I was so young and at the game and in the tournaments and all. But they quit calling me Junior when I began to beat them regularly. Minnesota Fats says everyone has to have a nickname. I guess if I have to, you'd have to call me 'Fast Eddie.' They used to call me that before, once in a while.

I just hope that I don't get that 'Second-Place Finish' jinx that Cowboy Jimmy Moore used to have. Second in everything. I think, that with me, it'll be all or nothing. I get too keyed about those final games.

"When I won that Stardust tournament in Las Vegas, they said that I was a 'Dark House.' I didn't think that I was a dark horse. That really burned me. I was expecting to take the whole thing anyway.

"I've got another thing here lately. I'm a partner in Charley's Cue and Cushion, a 30-table billiards parlor in Norwalk, California. I get 35 percent and a 150 dollars a week. I wouldn't do it for less. I live on 150 a week, at least. There are a few problems now—the tables for one. I don't remember what kind they are, but I don't like 'em. There are a couple of other problems too, but I'll get them taken care of when I get the time to spare.

"I like California. I like to live there and raise my family there and everything. I play golf with some of the movie stars and some of the stars play pool with me. I play a lot with Telly Sevalas. Vince Edwards likes pool, but can't play very well. Dean Chance plays a lot but I haven't played with him—some of the others have, though."

Ronnie has some favorites among the professionals. "The main thing is Eddy Kelly. Naturally he thinks that he is the best. All the pros think they are. I guess you really have to think you are the best. Kelly thinks he is. I think I am. So it gets down to who's the best. I have a lot of respect for Kelly.

"I don't discount any of the regulars. Not even the older ones. You can look at any of the tournaments. All you see—all the names—up there by themselves—Irving Crane and Luther Lassiter. I wouldn't discount any of 'em. Not at all. Even the stable ones who only play a good game of straight pool. They are all dangerous in a tournament.

"But two of the most colorful characters in the game —hell, in any professional sport—are Cornbread Red and U. J. Puckett. They are just outta sight. I'd pay $100 a week, just to be around them. But as far as getting down to the last man—I'd go with Eddy Kelly. Kinda looks like that."

Ronnie Allen has a long way to go. He has years and years of tournament pool ahead of him. At 29, he's already far ahead of most players. He's remarkable for his age. But the regulars don't call him "Junior" anymore. If they call him anything printable, they'd have to call him "Fast Eddie" or double-fast Ronnie or something. He's that good.

He might even be the sports next leader—in a few years.

# 2
# *Tom Kollins – the Dee Jay*

It takes courage to quit a $225 a week job to make a living at pool, especially when there are seven children at home, but Tom Kollins of Wayne, Michigan has done it and it works.

"There should be more tournaments—that's the thing," Kollins says. "There should be more of them. Right now it's double-tough to make a living at it. When I go out of town to a tournament, I have to drive and stay two or three nights and pay all my expenses. Then if I don't place first, I'm lucky to get $150. It's a tough way to go.

"But I've been doing it for the last two and a half years now—it's been that long since I quit at WCAR radio in Detroit and, as I said then, 'either take it or leave it'—do what you want to or not."

His record shows that he likes it. In May of 1966 he successfully defended his Michigan State championship at Joe Farhat's Velvet Rail in Lansing, Michigan. That gave him a chance to go to the Billiards Congress of America Open Tournament held that year in St. Louis. In the B.C.A. tournament he met an old friend—Joe Balsis.

"Balsis and I are old Pennsylvanians," Kollins says. "I come from Shamokin, down in the coal country. That's just 18 miles from Minersville, where Balsis is from. We know some of the same people there. But we never met in

Tom Kollins, former disk jockey.

Pennsylvania. I left in 1961 for Detroit and Balsis began playing again in 1963. He wasn't a player when I lived there—I never knew about him. As far as that goes, nobody ever knew him until he decided to play again and beat every living human being.

"At the B.C.A. tournament in St. Louis, I was leading Balsis 134–58. I missed a break shot and he got up and ran over 85 balls and beat me. That's how I now know Mr. Balsis."

Kollins knows a lot of the others in the game too. "Just before the Chicago Nationals (The B.C.A. the year before was held in Chicago), Jimmy Moore came to Detroit for an exhibition. I beat him there. In the nationals, I drew Jimmy. He ran 76 balls and scratched. I ran 27, Jimmy ran ten and made a safety. I couldn't do anything —then he ran 65 to win. In three innings!"

"Jimmy says that he was really out to get me after I beat him in Detroit. He said that he just wouldn't let me beat him again—especially in the nationals."

The Jansco's Johnston City tournament is Kollins's favorite.

"I didn't do well there last year (1967), because it's the first time I've played there. Didn't have much luck. But I liked the atmosphere. I lived with a few of the older men—Marcel Camp, Al Koslosky and some of the others. The guys who were playing the game over 30 years ago. I heard so many stories—great stories—about what Greenleaf and others used to do. Those older guys have fantastic memories. They not only remember the men who played 30 years ago, but they remember the number of balls that Greenleaf ran in '28. They really poured on the color for me. I loved to hear them talk.

"Johnston City isn't the biggest prize money tournament—the Las Vegas tournament is bigger. I think it's $30,000 and there is more back room action there. But I've never been there. It's the problem of when you're working you can't get off to go and when you're not working—you maybe can't afford it. I'm planning to make it this year.

"Buddy Hackett tells a great story about his manager booking him into the Catskills at $65 a week and he couldn't even live on that. He called his manager and said so. The manager said 'Buddy, you have to save up for those jobs.' So I'm saving up for Las Vegas and looking forward to it.

"Whenever I hear of a tournament, I like to go, if I can. The great thing about this work on the side that I'm doing now is—if I want to work, I can and if not, I don't have to. I do films and modeling on the side. It isn't Hollywood, but the pay is good—great.

"After I quit at WCAR radio, I got a call. They needed a pool player for a film that General Motors was making, so I did the thing for them. It wasn't much and I liked it. I was told that I ought to register with an agent. So now I'm doing films and things—promotional films—company productions—things like that. Newspaper and magazine modeling. I get $20 an hour for modeling and $100 a day for the films. Plus I do exhibitions now and then.

"I couldn't have done it without my wife Dolores. I guess she'd rather that I had a steady job, but I think she realizes that I like what I'm doing. She's very understanding.

"If it wasn't for her, I couldn't make it. She's got a real estate license and every few days she goes and sells a house. That really helps."

The Kollins family now includes Joe, 12, Tommy, 11, Rita, 10, Danny, 8, Anita, 7, Bonnie, 6, and Teresa, 4. It's a houseful.

"Tommy's the good one. He was fourth in the State Junior Billiards Tournament. He won the boys 11-year-old bracket, and when they put him in with the older kids—the 16-year-olds—he was fourth. He ran 17 balls and has a real nice stroke. Joe Farhat, owner of the Velvet Rail billiards parlor in Lansing, wants me to enter Tommy in the next Michigan State Tournament, but the entry fee is $35 and that's too much."

Kollins didn't start his playing that young. He was 15.

"I had a paper route and one of the deliveries was at the local billiards room. After a while I began to watch. Then I began to play a game or two. After a while, the people who got the next paper began getting it later and later. They had to wait because I was playing pool.

"It took me three years to learn to run 50 balls. The improvement is slower after that.

"My first tournament win was the Chamberburg, Pennsylvania city tournament in 1958. I've won small tournaments since then, but there has never been any cash involved in any of them except this last one—the Michigan State championship. I got $350 for that—oh, yes, I got $150 for second place at the Detroit Metropolitan tournament, placing behind Alton 'Babyface' Whitlow."

Kollins has a lot of opinions about billiards and billiards players.

"First, I think the emphasis on 'family billiard centers' is a good idea. It really helps the image of the game. It's getting so you might even see a man of the cloth in one of those 'family centers.'

"I don't like the hustling. There are a lot of players who play tournament speed, but don't play in the tournaments. They just don't need the advertising. It's just too bad. There should be enough in tournaments to eliminate the back room action. There's the big IF—if the money were bigger.

"Irving Crane is, I think, the class of billiards as long as Mosconi isn't playing. But there are a lot of good players coming up—Dallas West, whom I've played in regionals, Richie Florence from California. Some of the guys who have seen him say that he's got to be the next champion at the game. Eddy Kelly—there are just plenty of younger ones. Pete Margo from Union City, New Jersey, Steve Mizerak, a hotshot—there are others . . .

"I don't like to hustle. I just don't like it. Hustling

under tournament conditions would be OK, but as soon as you start winning, the guy'll change the game and you'll have to spot him something to make the game. Hustling under tournament conditions would be nice— when the guy missed, he shuts up and sits down. That'd be OK, but the usual conditions are miserable. I just like to play tournaments. It'd be real nice to play without the hustling. If you're a psychologist like Minnesota Fats and can con the guy, then you've got it made. Otherwise, it isn't easy and I'd rather not hustle at all. Some guys can, like Cornbread Red, for example. He thinks money is nothing but green stamps. He's got it or he hasn't. Doesn't mean a thing. I guess you have to be that way when you're working on several hundred a game or more —you can't think of it as money—it's just paper or something.

"I used to have time for golf. When I was working radio, all the stations I worked on before Detroit were smaller stations in Pennsylvania where you really had to do everything. I used to get out before the show and after and play golf. That was my all-consuming hobby— golf. I had a nine handicap—that's an average of 79–80 and I used to play all the time. That was before pool. Now I haven't played in months.

"My kids all follow me when I play in regional tournaments—they're right there. Joey, especially. The first time I won the Michigan State championship they gave me a table. I have it in the basement and the kids play on it. I seldom use it. They have all their friends in to play. And they really root for me. At Lansing, Joey ran into the men's room, into one of the stalls and said a prayer for me. All the kids are getting cues like mine for Christmas—three cues for three boys—and that'll mean they'll be on the table all the time. Dolores got one too. It'll be the best Christmas the boys ever had.

"I seldom play on a 5 x 10 table. Very rarely. I played

recently and pulled down some action. One of the guys said 'that big box doesn't slow you down any'—I guess it didn't but I wasn't used to it.

"Everybody hustles when you get right down to it. There shouldn't be anything wrong with hustling. It depends on how you look at it. I have a friend who is a contractor and he admits he hustles for customers and everything. Everybody does it.

"They used to call me the DeeJay, when I was working in radio. Now I don't think I have a nickname.

"I have played straight and nine-ball ever since I can remember. I just picked up one-pocket last year. As far as I'm concerned, it has to be 'the' game.

"But the big thing is tournaments. There is just not enough of them with enough good prize money. At Michigan I got the table the kids use. That's fine but a billiards table doesn't pay the rent. Now we've talked them into giving cash and all the guys like it better. There ought to be more money and guarantees too. Now you have to finish first in all those smaller regional tournaments just to pay the rent. If there were tournaments with a $1,000 first prize—one of them every week—then all the guys could make a decent living.

"I've been told that if I need to, I could always get back into radio. The agent that handles my film work says he could get me a good radio job next week if I need it, but that'll be later. The Las Vegas tournament is next and all. Maybe sooner or later, I'll get a billiards room, as most of the guys do.

"I'll go back to radio if . . ."

# 3
# *Don Willis – The Unknown Lion*

"If I ever had to have someone else shoot pool for my life, win or lose, live or die," Wimpy Lassiter once said, "the man that I'd have shooting for me is Don Willis."

Lassiter should know. He and Willis traveled together for 15 years, back and forth across the country shooting pool. They never had their own cue sticks. They always used house cues. And they never had to resort to the tricks of the trade—lemoning or stalling—because as Willis says, "When you're as good as we were, you don't need all that. All you do is out-shoot everyone else."

Yet among players, Willis is a mystery. After all these years, some still didn't know him, except by reputation. People who know of Minnesota Fats and Wimpy Lassiter and some of the others have no idea that Willis was even around at the same time.

But he wants it that way. As he says, "limelight costs me money." So Lassiter and Fats get the headlines and get magazine articles done on "How I shoot" and Willis stays in the background.

He hasn't had a picture taken for publication since World War II.

He has been the greatest Wing-shot artist the game has ever had. The Wing-shot, probably the hardest of the trick shots, became a Willis specialty years ago. It means rolling a ball down the table and shooting and pocketing it as it rolls.

"They called me Wing-Shot Willie," Willis says. "My record is 42 in a row. I've done that twice—once recently —42."

They sometimes called him the Cincinnati Kid, too, he says. Willis plays cards also, like he plays pool—double-tough and he doesn't scare out.

"I was playing down south once and one guy yelled, 'Hey Cincinnati, cumhere!' The guy didn't know much about Ohio except Cincinnati, so I was 'The Cincinnati Kid.'

"That and Wing-shot Willie—they're all the nicknames I've had. I have 'em and I don't. Eddy Taylor has always been 'The Knoxville Bear,' but everyone calls him Eddy. I'm Don Willis. That's all, but I'm Wing-shot Willie or the Cincinnati Kid sometimes."

'The Cincinnati Kid' not withstanding, Willis has lived for years in Canton, Ohio. He rarely talks about his game and travels, but now he's semi-retired there and will look back now and then on pool and cards and traveling and Wimpy and hustling and Willis.

Willis doesn't talk like a hustler. He has a large and surprising vocabulary. It's a cross between the vernacular of the pool hustlers and the erudite speech of a community leader.

"That's one of the reasons why Dean Chance and Bo Belinsky are friends of mine," Willis laughed. "I met them several years ago and I guess they didn't know what to expect. They were used to thinking of pool players as stereotypes.

"What is missing with a lot of these pool players is sophistication. Some of them, I won't say which ones, are always looking for the next week's room rent. They live in walk-ups and cheap hotels. That's why the game has the bad image it has. Some of them are very irreputable.

"I compare some of them—those others—to Damon Runyon—some of them are very Damon Runyonesque," he explains. "No, I take that back, some of them are back-alley Runyonesque.

"But don't get me wrong—I don't knock any pool player. All of them are my friends. I get along with everyone. Even with Willis Mosconi who doesn't like *anyone*. I don't knock anyone. That's part of my reputation. I don't say anything against anyone."

The grime of the Canton, Ohio streets doesn't elate Willis any, especially in the winter, but as he began to talk more and more about billiards, he began to brighten. Little can conceal his love for the game and his friends.

"A few years ago, when Minnesota Fats began to gain popularity, all the other players were knocking him. They said he wasn't any good. They said other things like that. I never said that. They finally asked me what I thought of Fats and I said that I thought he was a gentleman and a great player—a champion—and Fats read that in print and cried, broke down and cried. He's very emotional. 'Don,' he said, 'you're the only one who said that.' It's true, I don't knock anyone.

"That's part of my reputation—I never criticize others, and they are all my friends.

"But I think my best friend is Wimpy Lassiter. What a team we were. We were together for 15 years. In 1959, he came to Canton and stayed a year. We practiced together and played together. We never had our own cues when we were out on the road. It used to be when you came into a new house with a cue under your arm, everyone'd say, 'who's this guy with the cue?' But everyone has a cue—every 12-year-old has his own.

"It didn't used to be like that. And we never had to lemon or stall either. We just out-shot everyone. We never lost either—never left town broke. Sure we were down low at times, but there was always someone else to play.

"Lassiter was the one who said I had the heart of a lion and I think that's the best thing anyone has said about me. It doesn't cost me a dime to compliment others—not a dime. To make Fats feel good. To help him when everyone else is knocking him. Lassiter thinks that way too. It didn't cost him anything to say that about me but he did. It didn't cost Dean Chance anything to say that I'm the best nine-ball player around. Not a thing.

"I began playing during the depression. Everyone was out of a job. Everyone. There were a lot of hustlers around, trying to make some money with the game. I got so I could beat them and I kept on playing. It got to be the greatest thing on earth.

"But there's a difference between the lions and the lambs—the money players and the 'fun' players. Most tournament players can't play for cash. What is a tournament? Lassiter is a real lion. Some play in tournaments, then when there's cash on the table, they can't make a shot. That's the big difference, I guess. I don't play tournaments. Never have. I might now, in a few years, two or three. I might go down to Johnston City like Wimpy does. Or to Las Vegas to the tournament there."

Willis turns to pro football, remembering the Pro Football Hall of Fame, the imposing modern museum of football in Canton.

"Football—pro football—I love it. Follow it all the time. Bob Waterfield, the great back for the Los Angeles Rams is a protege of mine. He's a pool buff. I showed him how to play. He's in the Hall of Fame now. Dan Reeves, the owner of the Rams is a friend of mine too. They're two of my best friends."

In a suit and overcoat, Willis looks like some prosperous Canton merchant. At 59, he's a little out of shape, but the build is still there. If you look at him right, you'll realize that he has been an athlete.

"I played semi-pro ball around here years ago," he says. "I went to Canton Timken High then and played shortstop, forward in basketball, and halfback in football. The good

## Don Willis — The Unknown Lion 39

semi-pro teams then were the Nolan Coals and the McKinley A.C. That was in 1928 and 1929.

"There was no premium on height then, for basketball players. You could be a quick little man and do alright. I was a pretty clever player.

"I was pretty good at shooting longs and shorts. And running backwards . . ."

Willis laughs, thinking about it—years ago.

"Running backwards. I could beat anyone running backwards. We'd race a hundred yards and I'd give them 10 or 20 yards and still win. Backwards. I was a champ at that."

Willis was serious for a moment. "This isn't a question of bragging. Or being too egotistical. You have to be confident. A lot of pool players are nothing but braggadocio. You have to be confident. You have to have confidence in your secret heart, I mean.

"I have to live here in Canton. If others around here read stuff that isn't the truth, what'll they think of me?

"What about the movie *The Hustler?*"

"Jackie Gleason and Paul Newman (the stars) are both professionals. They could pass my muster. I'm pretty discerning. They are good. Pretty good. Gleason did his own shooting. I guess that Newman was good or Mosconi was good for him. Either way, that film was the renaissance of pool."

Willis considers his year and one-half year-old Oldsmobile. "This is a good car. I had thought about getting a new one, but why bother. This one's just as good as brand new. My wife has one like it too. Same make, same model."

In the trunk of the car, Willis thought he'd find some old clippings. He rummaged around in the trunk, pulling and twisting boxes of clothes. "My wife saves clothes or something and she gives away these clothes," he said, referring to the cardboard boxes in the trunk. "My wife never had to work. I was always a pretty good provider. We've got six children, all grown up by now. All live in this area of Ohio. Five daughters. The oldest is 39. And one son, Don Jr. He's a sign painter here in Canton and is good at it. Has his own shop.

"Here they are," he said, pulling old newspapers and sheets of paper out of the trunk. There on the yellowed sheets were the quotes and scores:

Jimmy Moore—one of the top players of all time. "In thirty-five years I lost only once for money. I lost to Don Willis in Louisville, Ky."

(The late) Harold Worst, Worlds Champion Three cushion player in *Sports Illustrated*, March 20, 1961— "Don Willis in my opinion is the best nine-ball player in the world."

Al Coslosky, veteran Pennsylvania player who won the World nine-ball title a few years ago says, "Every Worlds Tournament I attended Willis had an open challenge to play anybody."

And from the files of the Canton, Ohio, *Repository*:

| | |
|---|---|
| Erwin Rudolph | 35 |
| Don Willis | 125 |
| (high run Willis | 88) |
| Bobby Moore | 33 |
| Don Willis | 125 |
| (high run Willis | 48) |
| James Caras | 97 |
| Don Willis | 100 |
| (high run Willis | 87—unfinished) |
| Ralph Greenleaf | 40 |
| Don Willis | 125 |
| (high run Willis | 66—unfinished) |

| | |
|---|---|
| Willie Mosconi | 65 |
| Don Willis | 125 |
| (high run Willis | 70—unfinished) |

And a hand-out, a press release from a new billiard room, "The Golden Cue," in Bloomington, Minnesota, owned in part by Dean Chance:

> 'The likeable chubby Willis is famed throughout the world for his wing shots or as he says: "My duck hunting trips." He's an accomplished juggler using the table cushion for feats.'

"Hell," Willis snorts at that, "don't say I'm chubby. I'm not. I'm 240 pounds now and five feet eight and a half. That's not chubby or shorty, as I'd been called."

He laughs again. "That juggling. A gimmick. Yeh, I can juggle three balls and the chalk at the same time. I can shoot on the floor too. On the linoleum. I'm accurate even at 60–70 feet."

"Sure, I've even won bets on the proposition that I can't name in order the 130 largest cities of the U. S. There are 130 cities over 100,000 population. It's easy.

"I used to do a lot of things like that. Once ran 126 in straight pool. Beat Jimmy McClure who was then the World's Table Tennis champion. Beat him for money. I played him in Canton, Indianapolis, and Canton again. Also beat George May, who was then the world's horseshoe champion.

"I used to play three cushion billiards too. I was the only billiards player who could figure a four horse parlay in his head. It's a gimmick, just like memorizing the 130 cities."

Willis begins talking about the current players. "Handsome Danny Jones? Sure, he's a good friend of mine. He's up and coming. I went with him to the New York Tournament in 1967.

"Jimmy Moore? He was the best all-around player a few years back. Weenie Beenie Staton—yes, I like him very much. Eddie Kelly, Red Breit, like them too. Eddy Taylor, Wimpy Lassiter."

He thought of the time he was playing—playing who? —well, playing somebody and the guy said, "I wish Don Willis was here, he could beat you as bad as you're beating me now."

Willis said, "I wouldn't play him."

"There was another time I was playing and the guy said, 'You must be Don Willis, nobody else could beat me this badly.' That was good logic on his part, I just left."

"Without telling him?"

"Yes. Someone once wrote that I won sums like telephone numbers," Willis laughs again at this, "like telephone numbers. Then someone else added 'with area codes'—that really tops it!

"Pool has to excite you. It used to really excite me. I never practiced just for the sake of practicing. I always wanted to play—to play someone. That was it. I lived well on the game. I still do. I'm not so interested in it anymore. One guy around here has always seen me just sitting around or having a drink or something—never working—and he finally said, 'What do you do for a living?' and I said, 'Sit around.' He believed it—that was all he had ever seen me do.

"Now and then my friends call me and tell me to come to Kansas City or some place and play a youngster who think's he's the best there is. I do it. Not very often anymore. Once every few months or so. Yeh, I know them all, the pros and the fun players.

"I guess if you had to sum it up, you could say that I'd rather play Joe Blow for $7, than the World's Champion for nothing."

"That sounds good. Yeh, that's it. I'd rather play anyone for $7 than the World's Champion for the fun of it."

# 4
# U. J. Puckett – Mr. One-Pocket

If you ask Ronnie Allen who the best one-pocket pool player is, he'll probably answer U. J. Puckett.

Puckett will probably admit it too.

"I didn't play straight billiards until just three years ago," Puckett says. "Years ago when I learned, one-pocket was what everyone played. No one in Texas was playing straight pool because they thought it wasn't a good game. They bet on it in New York, but in Texas everyone stuck with one-pocket and nine-ball. I think it was better that way. One-pocket players can play straight pool if they want to, but straight pool players can't necessarily play one-pocket.

"Look at Balsis. Look at Irving Crane. Crane has never beaten me. I played him one-pocket three times and he never won one game. In Las Vegas a year ago, I played Balsis one-pocket and he lost four straight games. Lassiter too. They can't beat me at one-pocket. It's all in knowing what to do.

"But I'm beginning to like straight pool and I'm improving at it."

As proof of his one-pocket distinction, Puckett was in the top few in one-pocket at the Jansco's Johnston City competition. The last tournament that Puckett won was the 1960 Macon, Georgia National Nine-Ball on March 19, 1960. He had to beat Danny Jones and Eddy Taylor to get to the title.

U. J. Puckett, Mr. One-Pocket.

He is, in his own words, the best player in the southwest.

"We do need more tournaments though. The prize money is getting there. In a few years you could make a good living at it. But now for the 25–30 regulars at the tournaments, you need a few more than the five or six big tournaments a year.

"But I make enough at it to fish and hunt. Hunt for quail and fish for black bass. Yes, yes.

"Minnesota Fats was talking to me the other day and he said that we ought to go into partnership and get a billiards room in Dallas or Fort Worth. Mebbe we'll do that—that'd give me more time to hunt and fish.

"Fats and I are good friends. I was on his TV show in Chicago. It's $1,000 if you win and $600 if you lose. I didn't let him beat me, he just did. Fats won one game, I won one, and Fats got the $1,000 because he was ahead when the time ran out for the show.

"I've been playing since I was 15 and I'm 62 now. I'll bet anyone $10 that I have been in their home town to play. I seldom lose that bet. I've been everywhere. You name the place and I've played someone there.

"From Johnston City I may spend the winter in Florida. I play a lot in Miami but I've been to the Bahamas, Honolulu, and I've played in Mexico and Canada.

"They have an interesting game in Mexico. They call it Mexican Rotation. You freeze all the balls on the diamonds and shoot in rotation. In Cuba they call it 'Chicago.' It's a very tricky game. Usually, if I play it, I'll spot my opponent the 12-ball.

"Billiards is like wrasslin'. There are all sorts of champions. Everywhere you go, you'll find someone who'll tell you he's champ. Usually on those itty-bitty 3 x 6 foot bar tables. Especially in California. Everyone there is a bar champ. It's a paradise for pool.

"But I'm like all the rest—I'll tell you I'm the champ.

"I'll play with anybody, but favorites are Eddy Taylor —'The Knoxville Bear'—and Cornbread Red and Eddy Kelly. Red and Kelly are two of the best.

"You know, I named Taylor, 'The Knoxville Bear.' I did. He and I were playing and he beat me and beat me and beat me. I finally said that I'd rather tangle with one of them Smokey Mountain bears. We were playing in

U. J. Puckett and Eddy "The Knoxville Bear" Taylor.

Knoxville, Tennessee at the time. After that, people called him The Knoxville Bear.

"I never did get any particular nickname except my initials. Minnesota Fats would pronounce them Uuuuuuuu-uJay, as though I was a big business executive or something. So I've always been U. J. Everybody knows me as U. J.

"Yes, ole U. J. is the best one-pocket player in the world, but there are some others who aren't bad. Ronnie Allen, there. He's my favorite. Sooner or later, he'll be the best one-pocket player in the world. Eddy Kelly too. In a few years, Kelly'll be the best in nine-ball. Jack Breit is the best all-around player.

"Pool is fascinating. If I had to live my whole life over again, choose anything I like, I think that I would do exactly the same thing.

"No, I wouldn't either. I'd do more hunting and fishing."

Old U. J. still shoots a good stick. He won the Texas Open to qualify for the Johnston City tournament. He's placed in the money in the last five tournaments he's played in.

But the one thing he doesn't take kindly to is calling him by his real name—Utley John.

# 5

## *Sonny Springer – The Southern Gentleman*

T. J. "Sonny" Springer has been playing billiards for as long as he can remember. "I don't know what it is *not* to play. I guess I've always played billiards. I remember having to stand on a coke case just to get at the table. It's like being born afflicted. People have asked me how long I've been playing. I don't know any different—I've always played.

"My father has always had a billiards room. I guess he taught me to play. He still has one.

"Now and then he'll say something about my playing, like 'he has to know how to play, he knows what I know and what he has learned on his own'—statements like that. But a man's only young once and he has to do what he likes to do."

Doing what he likes to do means, for Springer, playing as much as he can at home and taking time off to get to the B.C.A. Opens and the Johnston City soirée.

"I was 15th in the B.C.A. Open in St. Louis and came in fourth in the Columbus, Georgia, National. I was 17th in the Las Vegas tournament year before last and ninth in Johnston City last year. I haven't entered *many* national tournaments, but I've been in the money in all of them."

He is the current Mississippi state champion. He won that title in May of 1967 in Jackson, Mississippi. And he

Tex Jean "Sonny" Springer.

won it playing his weakest game—straight pool. But he waded through more than 30 competitors for the title.

"One-pocket is my best game. And straight is my weakest. I just don't play it. Down in Mississippi no one plays it."

To put groceries on the family table, Sonny and his father, J. E. Springer own the Springer Lime Fertilizer Company, in Mantee, Mississippi. It was a big business before and is now bigger—they bought out a local co-op and quadrupled their business.

"I plan to get away for these tournaments—but business is good. Spring and fall are our busy seasons, the planting season and the fall, when the crops are in. Everyone fertilizes then."

Sonny's family includes his wife Ursula—"Hikie"—and Tommy, 15, and Tammy, six. The Springers have been married 19 years.

"Tommy shoots a good game himself," Sonny says. "We're adding another room to the house for a billiards table. I have to play on the $4\frac{1}{2}$ x 9 foot tables at the tournaments and the only thing I play on at home is the 4 x 8 foot tables. So I'm building on another room and will put in a new $4\frac{1}{2}$ x 9 table.

"Usually I come to the tournaments cold. At the most, I get one or two days practice. I think I do exceptionally well for as much practice as I have."

Springer's southern accent is as heavy as a slate table. He speaks so softly at times you can hardly hear him. He has a wry view of hustling and success. Four miles from his home, down the road, is the home of Bobby Gentry, whose record "Ode to Billie Joe" hit the tops of the teeny-boppers' record charts and stayed there. Her soft tale of southern horror in the Faulknerian, gothic tradition is hardly a model for the "new South." And, like pool players, she's a hustler of sorts too. Her name isn't Bobby Gentry, it's Billie Jean Streeter.

Forgetting her success with that one record, Springer turns again to pool.

"I enjoy these places, really enjoy them. I like to watch U. J. Puckett, especially in the tournament games. He complains and carries on so, especially when he's losing.

"My wife goes along with the idea that occasionally I have to get to a tournament. I just get that urge and have to go. This Johnston City tournament is better this year. If a man draws well, he could place high. It depends on his bracket. Several games stand out in my mind recently. I was playing Danny DeLiberto one-pocket and had only two balls to go. I mis-cued. And it was a new cue—he beat me.

"I also played Minnesota Fats. We were both playing terrible pool but I was playing worse and there was a

T. J. "Sonny" Springer.

little money on the table. I lost. Fats knows all the angles and he's double tough."

Springer has had the nickname "Sonny" for so long that he can't remember now where he got it. He does remember that he doesn't like his given name "Tex Jeans."

"I was named after a baseball player Daddy liked. But I've never used these names. I've always been Sonny."

Sonny is ambidextrous. He shoots left-handed billiards, but uses his right more often. He can drive a nail with both hands and saw lumber with both hands.

"I know that I am stronger in my right hand, but I shoot billiards with my left. Don't know why . . ."

The next time Sonny Springer gets to a tournament, keep an eye on him.

After all, the South will rise again.

# 6
# *William Burge – Cornbread Red*

U. J. Puckett thinks that "Cornbread Red" Burge is the funniest man alive. He laughs just thinking of Red.

"He looks like a little hawk. Just like a little sparrow hawk," Puckett says. But ol' U. J. hesitates a little when it comes to playing Red, especially if there is some money on the game. Red has been in the game a long time—17 years, at least—and he's considered one of the best. He doesn't scare out of any action for any stakes.

"Billiards is the only thing I've ever done," Red says, "I've never worked at anything else. I've been across the country, from coast to coast. Usually I'll drive, but I have flown to a match. I'll play with anybody.

"One-pocket is my best game. I play straight a little bit. But a lot of guys don't play it and you have to play what the rest are playing.

"I used to play a lot of snooker too. But I'll play *any* game with *anyone*. My favorites are Ronnie Allen and Eddy Kelly. Yeh, I guess that's right. Allen and Kelly. They're good boys. I'll play with Minnesota Fats too. I was on his TV show July 3, 1967. Shut him out, beat him bad."

If you pin him down, Red will admit that he wins and loses a lot on the tables. He also wins and loses at craps in Las Vegas. During the 1967 tournament in Las Vegas, for a week or so, Red won at pool and he won at craps. When he stopped to add up the bills, he had won $90,000,

Bill "Cornbread Red" Burge.

give or take a few dollars. But because Red thinks so little of money, he gave other hustlers new clothes, new shoes, he tipped lavishly, and went on gambling.

A couple of days later he was broke. The $90,000 had nearly disappeared. There was a little left, but it was hardly worth mentioning after that big win.

Even a couple thousand he had put on a part-ownership

of a billiards room in Florida was gone. Red had called Florida, got his investment out of the room and put it back on the tables. He left town "mighty low" as one hustler put it. "The trouble with Red," he added, "is that he thinks of money as Green Stamps. Either he has it or he doesn't. That's all."

Red's case might be painful but it is true and his utter disregard for what money is and what it can do is one of the chief characteristics of the hustler mentality. Money is no big thing to him.

"I guess I am known as a comedian" Red says. "I can blow a lot—really bad—and I don't care about it. Other guys, you take their money and they really want to get at you. They actually want to kill you. I don't care that much."

Red has a wife and three children in Highland Park, Michigan.

"My wife Ellen is OK about my playing. Except when I'm gone for a month or so. A week to ten days is fine but longer than that, she doesn't like."

One of the chief amusements at Johnston City in 1968 was Red's inability to remember the name of one of his children.

"I have three girls," he'd say, "Carol is six and a-half. Leslie is three and one-half and—lemme see—what is the third?"

Red's bad memory was excusable. His third daughter was born just before the Johnston City tournament, the highlight of Red's pool year. He was almost too busy on the tables, on the tournament action and the back-room stuff to get any sleep.

"Lemme think—yes, Claudia Lynn—she's two weeks old."

After 17 years at pool, Red does admit he has some second thoughts about the game. "If I had to do it all over again, I wouldn't get into billiards. No sir. I sure wouldn't.

The Lions and the Lambs 56

"Just like a little sparrow hawk," William "Cornbread Red" Burge.

It's a good game, but people think you're a bum. A hustler. And they think the game isn't any good. That's the reason I don't like the game. People just have the wrong idea about it. They think you're a bum and that's not right."

Red's disgust at the image of billiards in general is

usually short-lived. He's happy at the game and gets great enjoyment out of the other regulars.

"Ronnie Allen, Eddy Kelly. They sure are a pair. I guess I like to play with them better than anybody else. But that old U. J. Puckett. He's the funniest guy I know. Especially when he's losing. I'd as soon watch him as anyone."

Red laughs at the thought of watching Puckett's agonies. But ask anyone else and they'll probably say there isn't anyone funnier to watch than ole Cornbread Red. He kibitzes and jokes and laughs and occasionally blows a few easy shots. Given the right conditions, he won't hesitate to play a little nine-pocket for some money on one table with, say, Eddy Kelly and Ronnie Allen and, at the same time, try to beat a proposition shot—a set-up, with "Weenie Beenie" Billy Staton at another table at the same time. He did that at Johnston City to the vast amusement of the crowd and managed comfortable wins on both tables.

And it's all very funny. Red has the best time of them all. Especially when he's winning. And he wins a lot.

# 7
## Pete Margo – The Youngest Lion

In 1965, when Pete Margo was 19, he was conned into playing nine-ball with a stranger in New York. Margo and his opponent began playing early in the evening and when the billiards room was closed for the evening, Margo and the other player were even-up.

"It made me mad, when the owner closed the place for the evening," Margo said, "because I thought at the time that I could have beaten the guy."

It was well that Margo was forced to quit when he did, for "the guy" Margo was playing was "Handsome" Danny Jones, who was the nine-ball champion that year.

"I went back to the owner, after I found out who I had just played, and thanked him for closing when he did. I was just young enough not to realize who I was up against."

Not that Margo is much older now, but when you play the best at 19, there is no sense in being frightened away from the action when you are 24.

Pete Margo is probably the youngest player to regularly compete in national tournaments. And, as some other players know, Margo knows how to stack the action. He has taken down a lot from older, more experienced players because of his youth and his speed.

His home is Union City, New Jersey, a ten-minute trip through the Lincoln Tunnel from Manhattan. The career skyline of Manhattan is impressive from Union City, but

Pete Margo, one of the youngest lions in the game of pool.

Margo has already made the trip and scaled the heights.

In 1968, Pete qualified for the New York's World Championship, held in the Statler Hilton hotel. He was among the 36 qualifiers, but as the tournament began, he learned that his father, Danny Margaritonda, was dying of lung cancer.

"He told me that he wanted me to go and play," Pete

Pete Margo, outside Danny's Billiards, the Union City, New Jersey pool room owned by his father and now run by Pete.

says. During the tournament his father died and Pete, shaken, was 13th out of 15.

A year earlier, Pete was fifth in the straight pool division at the Jansco's Johnston City, Illinois tournament. He beat Bob Nolan, Shirley Cloyd, and Junior Golf, before losing to Irving Crane.

And at the 1967 B.C.A. Open in St. Louis, he beat U. J. Puckett before being beaten by Cisero Murphy. Margo had two runs of 45 each before Murphy ran 108-and-out.

Already known as an action player and a high-run specialist, Margo naturally appreciates the Johnston City style.

"It's ideal for gambling," he says. "I really like that all-night action. The tournament itself is expensive, but the back-room action is terrific."

Margo also likes the action in New York. "It's really a good pool area. You really have to prove yourself. It's tough to take down any kind of action in New York. You have to know your own speed and your opponents speed."

Unlike thousands of Manhattan and New Jersey residents who move to that area, Margo is a life-long resident. He graduated from Union City High School in 1963. He never went to college: "pool would have kept me too busy anyway."

Margo learned his game from his father. When Pete was 15, his father bought him a toy table. After only a few months, Pete was playing well on regulation tables. Eventually Mr. Margaritonda bought Danny's Billiards, an 8-table house on 38th Street in Union City.

After the death of his father, Pete has been running the room, aided by his mother. Pete has decorated the room with two-by-three foot large posters of players who have played there, plus a few of his own favorite actors and actresses. Irving Crane stares down from the walls, beside Lou "Machine Gun" Butera. Cisero Murphy is

Pete Margo lines up a shot.

there, beside Frank McGowan and Eddy Taylor. The comedian W. C. Fields hangs beside Cue Ball Kelly. The late Jayne Mansfield is shown in a low-cut gown, bending deliciously over a masse shot and Rudolph Valentino is there too, because "he's my favorite," Margo says.

"I owe everything to my father," says Margo. "He was a pretty good player who could have been better except he hurt his bridge hand early in life and could never shoot exactly right."

So now Pete runs the room and when he has to go to a tournament, his mother runs it. His sister Linda, 22, and his mother, Mrs. Marie Margaritonda are his two biggest fans, but occasionally Linda's loyalties are split. She has been dating Steve Mizerak and sometimes Pete and Steve are in the same tournament.

Part of Margo's play is dictated by his size. Eddy Taylor has suggested that he take Pete on the road, dress him up in a sweatshirt with a big block "T" for the University of Texas and match him against local players throughout Texas. Margo is cool to the idea: he'd rather play in the metropolitan tournaments around New York and occasionally give exhibitions or take on local lambs.

When he has to travel to tournaments like Johnston City, he'll stop along the way for a little action and road money. He used to play a lot in Columbus, Ohio, where "Handsome" Danny Jones had a room. With his diminutive size (he weighs about 115 pounds), he'd never be taken for a high speed player—especially in a college town—until others began to lose to him.

He has made runs of "200, 170, 155, 145—like that" in practice.

In the Cavalcade of Stars tournament, a traveling tournament lasting throughout the summer of 1968, Pete placed fourth, tied with Cisero Murphy and Mike Eufino. In the International, held at the Hotel Commodore in New York, he was a bit lower. The International featured 12 players from the U.S. and four players, one each from England, Japan, Australia, and Puerto Rico.

The Bunnies from the New York Playboy Club were the rack girls, to add a little class to the tournament, but whether they added class or were just distractions is a debatable point. Steve Mizerak was in the middle of a high run when he saw, through the corner of his eye, a bunny's cotton tail fall off. He was so sidetracked by the bounteous bunny that he missed the shot.

But Mizerak eventually was second and Margo was sixth. Pete's showing brought him $700, but the tournament, on the business side was a fiasco—money, the taproot of the lions' life, was slow in coming and there was a general hassle before the winners were paid.

In the B.C.A. Open, Margo did as well, but a little better. He won three early, easy games and lost one before beating Bill "Weenie Beenie" Staton 150–59. Then he drew Cisero Murphy and Cisero, cool as always, beat him 150–81 to end Pete's tournament matches. He was 14th out of 54 players and that earned him $300. He had a 6.55 balls-per-inning average—a bit low for a major tournament.

There is very little in the past of Pete Margo to chronicle, he is so young. He has a long way to go in the game and his speed and tournament records are bound to improve with the months and the coming years. Whether he shoots in his Union City room, or whether he bends over the tables in the famous rooms of the past—Ames in New York, Bensinger's in Chicago, Cochrane's in San Francisco—or even if he takes up Eddy Taylor's offer and plays in El Paso wearing a University of Texas sweatshirt, Margo *will* work his way into the pool world of bigger money and tournaments that are won, not lost.

Pete Margo.

# 8

## *Hustling in Johnston City*

For more than 11 months of the year, Johnston City, Illinois, population 3,900, is a forgotten farm town in the southern tip of Illinois just north of Cairo, in the section called "Little Egypt." And there are no easy roads to get there.

But for three weeks or so, during October and November of each year, it's a hustlers' paradise and non-hustlers who enter are stepping into the lions' den. It is easily the hustlers' capital of the world.

The pool tournament that is conducted there, the World's All-Around Pocket Billiards Tournament, is known as "The Hustler." There is plenty of action on the side and it is heavy and fast.

Prize money put up by the promoters of the tournament, George* and Joe Jansco of Johnston City, amounts to $20,000, split among three brackets, straight pool, one-pocket and nine-ball. But a decent hustler can make that much during the three weeks with the back room action, between tournament games.

Billiards gambling is an art. Most of the really big gambling now is on professional golf and Las Vegas-style games. There are only a few dozen men good enough to make a living with pool action.

---
\* George Jansco died suddenly Wednesday, June 4, 1969 of a cerebral hemorrhage. Whether or not the Johnston City tournaments will remain as well organized in the next few years is uncertain.

In attendance this year at various times were: "Wimpy" Lassiter; "The Knoxville Bear" Eddy Taylor; "Weenie Beenie" Staton; Cornbread Red; "Handsome Danny" Jones; "Boston Shorty" Larry Johnston; "The Squirrel" Marshall Carpenter; Irving Crane; Hubert "Danny Warbucks" Cokes; Minnesota Fats; Eddie Kelly; Ronnie Allen; Jack "The Red Raider" Breit; Martin "Omaha Fats" Kaiman; Sonny Springer; U. J. Puckett; Blackie LaSieur; Danny DiLiberto; Tom Cosmo; Cisero Murphy; Tom Kollins, and others.

The only players to miss the action this year (1968) were Joe Balsis, who had a heavy set of exhibition dates and Willie Mosconi, who is retired.

All the action happens in the "back room"—a squat, white cement block building behind the Jansco's Show Bar, which can be converted into a billiards room for the tournament. The door of the back room carried the ubiquitous sign "Cue Club of America—Members Only" and inside there is a row of bleachers along one wall for spectators and five pool tables. During the tournament, the tables are used constantly, sometimes 24 hours a day. Smoke hangs heavily in the room and conversation is sparse and low-key.

The problem with hustling in Johnston City is that the pros all know each other's ability—their speed—and thus must handicap each other to get up some good action.

So Weenie Beenie will spot Cornbread Red 4-1 or 5-1 that Red can't go "round the horn," complete a complicated trick shot involving setting all the balls in an L-shaped pattern and pocketing them all in one corner pocket. It isn't easy to explain—harder to shoot. Weenie Beenie will put the money on the table and Red and Cuban Joe and Ronnie Allen will give it a try. Usually Weenie Beenie will take their money. Occasionally one of them will make it and take the pile.

On another table, three or four or five hustlers will play

nine-ball hour after hour. This year five hustlers played nine-ball for $20 a game for 30 hours.

"Here," one hustler said to another, during a lull in the action, "gimme a hundred dollar bill for this garbage" ($100 in 10s and 20s). His buddy obliged.

The smallest bet at Johnston City is usually a $20 bill—bet on one shot. But as much as $300–400 changes hands among hustlers and spectators on one shot.

Total prize money on the tournament tables at Johnston City is $20,000. But hustlers, by staying up most of the night, night after night, can make that much and more in the back room. And since stamina is one prime prerequisite for a good pool player, that kind of money *is* made at Johnston City.

For the past few years, Johnston City action has been lent an aura of respectability because of television. The finals of the tournament play have been filmed by ABC's *Wide World of Sports*, for showing later. This has caused mixed feelings among the pros. The extra $8,000 that the television brings in is welcomed, but the exposure isn't.

"Once you've been seen on television, that's it," one hustler said. "You don't have much hope of hustling in a strange town when you've been seen on TV."

Stalling and lemoning, possible in other locations at different times, are not seen in Johnston City. The hustlers know each other too well and are sharp enough to spot a con.

Players wander in and out of the back room—out to get something to eat, to get some sleep, to play in their tournament matches or to find a backer for some more money. They wander in, after tournament games, to watch the action, joke with each other, to watch and make bets on the side, or to play. They all know each other; it's a family gathering, in a bizarre setting. Between the back room and the tournament action, the hustlers park their cars. They are all new, like Ronnie Allen's financed on the strength of his game, and they bear license plates from across the country: New York, Massachusetts, California, Mississippi, Michigan, Texas, Georgia, and Nevada.

Inside, day or night, the games go on—nine-ball, one-pocket, set-ups (propositions). Allen, Kelly, Red, Jack Breit, Omaha Fats, Jim Relihan, a young hustler called "The Springfield Rifle, from Springfield, Massachusetts, Daddy Warbucks—all are in and out; the games and the players change, but the action continues—Weenie Beenie, Puckett—they all take a turn at the tables, waiting, watching, betting, joking.

It's the lion's den—the world's best pool players. In Johnston City, Illinois, population 3,900. While it lasts, it's fastest pool action in the country.

## THE REST
## THE OTHER TOP PLAYERS IN PHOTOGRAPHS

The Lions and the Lambs 70

Jack Breit, sometimes called "The Red Raider" or "Jersey Red," is a dangerous money player. (Courtesy *National Bowlers Journal & Billiard Revue* magazine.

Jack "The Red Raider" Breit. (Courtesy Billiard Archives)

Jimmy Caras. (Courtesy Billiard Archives)

An early picture of Jimmy Caras. (Courtesy Billiard Archives)

An early picture of Irving "The Deacon" Crane. (Courtesy Billiard Archives)

The Lions and the Lambs 74

Richie Florence, a rising young shooter from California. (Courtesy Billiard Archives)

The late Willie Hoppe. (Courtesy Billiard Archives)

The late George Jansco (with cue ball), manager of the World's All-Around Pocket Billiard Tournament, and Luther Lassiter, one of the best players in the game and winner of five world titles in a six-year span. Behind trophy, wearing round glasses, is billiards showman Tom Cosmo. (Photo by *National Bowlers Journal* magazine)

Ed Kelly, one of the best younger players. (Courtesy Billiard Archives)

Willie Mosconi. For years the name Mosconi has meant "billiards" just like the name Babe Ruth means baseball. Before his retirement recently, Willie Mosconi was the man to beat at the game. (Courtesy Billiard Archives)

Cisero Murphy, the only Negro in big-time billiards.
(Courtesy Billiards Archives)

The late Charles C. Peterson, the father of intercollegiate billiards, particularly in the Big Ten universities. (Courtesy Billiard Archives)

"Weenie Beenie" Staton. (Courtesy Billiard Archives)

Eddy Taylor, "The Knoxville Bear." (Courtesy Billiard Archives)

Rudolph "Minnesota Fats" Wanderone. (Courtesy Billiard Archives)

Dallas West, young up-and-coming tournament winner from Rockford, Illinois. West, according to Ronnie Allen, has "the best break shot in the business." (Photo by National Bowlers Journal magazine)

*Part II*

# THE LAMBS

> . . . in pool, they are tournament winners, "fun players," who don't usually have the "heart" or courage to win when there is money on the game.

# 9
## Joe Balsis – The Next Mosconi

For years and years, during the reign of Willie Mosconi as champion of the pool world and then, following Mosconi's retirement and Luther Lassiter's reign, the name Joe Balsis was never mentioned in tournament news. Until 1963, Balsis was earning a living and supporting a family in Minersville, Pennsylvania, as owner of a chain of six meat markets, "Economy Joe's."

Balsis has the build of a butcher, or a coal miner. He has thick arms and legs, the heavy chest of a laborer, and short, stubby fingers. But in 1965, Balsis took off the butcher's apron, took his cue in hand, and risked his livelihood on tournament pool. His climb has been prodigious; in 28 months Balsis entered ten major tournaments, and won five championships—including the Billiard Room Proprietors' Association World's Championship in 1965, and the ABC TV National Invitational, also in 1965. He was runner-up in another, placed fourth in two of the ten tournaments, and fifth in another two. He has made a comfortable living on the game, and he was the man who challenged Mosconi, who came out of retirement to play in a California tournament in a billiards room named The House of Champions.

Billiards has always been a favorite in California, and pool counts among its followers Fred Astaire, Peter Falk, Mickey Rooney, James Garner, and baseball star Dean

Joe Balsis, the Minersville Butcher, shoots during an exhibition. Balsis spends considerable time giving exhibitions in colleges, sports goods shows, and other events. (Photo by Dave Luck)

Chance. So in April of 1966, a promoter named Arnie Satin offered Mosconi a guarantee of $10,000 and a percentage of the profits to enter his tournament in The House of Champions. It really looked like Mosconi would take the whole show—he was steady, smooth and showed his old form. He beat his first seven opponents easily, then lost to Cisero Murphy, a young Negro player from New

Joe "The Butcher" Balsis with one of his many trophies.
(Courtesy Billiard Archives)

York. Mosconi won his next six matches but was again beaten by Irving Crane, 150–84. Mosconi was so rattled by that loss he chased Satin out the door swearing, which was not the usual Mosconi temperament. While Mosconi was winning and then dropping the two matches, Balsis was winning his last seven matches of the tournament, after two early losses. Balsis came to the show-down with Mosconi unimpressed with Willie's 13 world titles. On the tables, facing Mosconi's suave coolness, Balsis won, 150–93. Mosconi resolved then never to play in another tournament.

The victory was especially good for Balsis. Not only did he beat the great Willie, but he also locked up the tournament with the tournament's high run, 137 balls, and best game, a win in two innings. He also took from Mosconi the official record of balls-per-inning average of 22, beating Mosconi's old record of 18.34, set in the 1950 World's Tournament.

Balsis also won $4,000 and Mosconi, temperamental and humiliated, refused to appear in the winning ceremonies to take his runner's-up check for $3,000.

Suddenly Balsis was the man-who-beat-the-champ. But he was no rookie at the game. He had been playing on and off, winning a few titles years before, playing now and again in Minersville, and trying to decide whether or not to give up the meat business.

It was the final step in Balsis' return to pool, the game that gave him a small trophy as 1932 winner of the Philadelphia City Boys' tournament and the Armed Forces championship in 1944. At 12, he ran 87 balls to win the National Junior Championship. But he had started sooner than that. He began the game when he was four and his father had to lift him up to the table.

"My father ran a good room in Minersville," Balsis remembers. "He put me onto the table and let me go. It was always a great place—never any trouble. It was the best room around. He still has a room today, by the way. But when I was in high school, I was practicing seven to nine hours a day and he had to chase me off the tables and out the door." He managed to also play linebacker for Minersville High School at the same time. But after that, there was the Army championship and then the meat markets. And marriage to Eleanor Radzievich, also a Minersville native. Putting food on the

Joe Balsis surveys a difficult shot during a recent exhibition at the University of Iowa, Iowa City. (Photo by Dave Luck)

table for the Balsis children came first, and pool, during the years from 1946-1963, was a dream.

But then, after a long talk with Eleanor, and a belief that maybe he could make a living in tournament pool without hustling, he began. In 1964, his first year of tournament play since the Armed Forces championship, he placed fourth in the Billiard Room Proprietors' Association, (BRPA) World's Championship Tournament in New York City. On his second try the next year, he won that tournament, won the New York State Open, won the National Invitational, and placed fifth in the Burbank, California Invitational.

In 1966 he won the Long Beach, California Invitational, won the Burbank Invitational, and placed fifth in the BRPA tournament. In 1967, he won the Culver City, California Invitational, the CBS-TV Classic, beat Eddy Kelly in the Jansco's World's All-Around Tournament in Johnston City, Illinois, and placed seventh in the Billiard Congress of America Tournament.

In 1968 he won the Las Vegas Stardust Tournament. And he came back the next year and won the Stardust again in 1969.

It all means money to feed the Balsis family. Just how much, Joe won't say. "If I do, the boys from IRS (Internal Revenue) will start coming around," he says.

The win at Johnston City, the hustlers capital, means as much to Balsis as anything else. The year before, in the B.C.A. championships, he and Irving Crane got off to a slow start in the finals, each playing safeties. Then Crane got hot, took charge, and ran out in a little over an hour to beat Balsis 150-0. The second-prize of $1,500 was little psychological reward. But in Johnston City, Balsis picked up his cue, and ran out on Crane, 150-0 in the semi-finals. Crane got into the finals beating Eddy Kelly, 150-3, but again Balsis beat him, 150-0.

The atmosphere at Johnston City doesn't agree with

## Joe Balsis — The Next Mosconi

Balsis. There the hustlers are kings, and some go home broke. Not Balsis. The money he wins, he makes on the tournament tables. "I never hustle," he says, "because I don't like to think that I have ever taken money from anyone who has to support a family at home." And he never has.

Between tournaments now, he is a member of the Brunswick Advisory staff, traveling around the country, giving exhibitions in department stores, sporting good shows, and colleges. He likes the college and university audiences best. "I really enjoy it. I like to meet the students. They are a very appreciative audience. They share my exhibitions with me. When I miss a shot, the kids feel as badly as I do." An average exhibition schedule for Balsis is one with stops in Iowa, then a plane to Reno, Nevada, then Sacramento and Los Angeles, Las Vegas for two weeks, San Francisco for a week, Salt Lake City, and back to Chicago.

Balsis is a confirmed lamb. Other players claim that there isn't really a contest unless there is money on the table. Balsis doesn't believe that. "If you're playing for money and lose, you can say 'rack 'em up again.' But you can't in a tournament. There is no game again. You win or lose." The best tournament for this kind of pressure is the New York State Open. It's the symbol of championship pressure. It is pool à la carte."

Balsis, like many others in the game deplores the lack of any real money in the few tournaments that are scheduled each year. He knows more about it than most, with his connections with the Brunswick company. "There are few tournaments because there is very little to merchandise in pool, especially compared to golf. There you have to have shoes, balls, clubs and a bag. Even in bowling you have to have a bag and shoes. All you need for a game of pool is a stick and you don't have to buy that —you can use a house stick. If there would be more tour-

A painful miss by Joe Balsis. (Photo by Dave Luck)

naments, the promoters would naturally benefit and the manufacturers would also benefit."

And the others in the game?: Don Willis—"he's very good. He has a fine juggling act and of course, he's known for his wing-shots. He's underrated because no one knows him."

Minnesota Fats: "He's OK in his own way. He makes money in his own subtle way. The game needs men like that, but it can be overdone; the nicknames and his whole style of play."

"Weenie Beenie" Staton: "He's a clutch player for

the money. He doesn't win many tournaments—I've heard it said that he'd give his right arm for a big tournament win. That's probably true."

Bob Froeschle, B.C.A. tournament director: "Froeschle is the most underestimated person in the game. He knows *how* to get everyone together playing smoothly. He's misunderstood sometimes, but he always has control of the situation. We (players) need him in the game. I'm proud to say that I know him well."

Eddy Kelly is one of Balsis's favorites. Balsis beat Kelly in the Jansco's Johnston City matches in 1966, but actually wanted Kelly to win. "I've won titles before, and one extra doesn't mean that much. But a title like that would have done a lot for Kelly. I actually wanted him to win."

When Balsis gets home to Minersville, in between tournaments and exhibitions and travels, he joins Eleanor and their three children. Their daughter, Eleanor, attends Moore College; Joe Jr. is in Minersville High School, following his father by playing football and shooting for college competition in pool; John is beginning grade school. The Balsis family lives in a converted doctor's office. The doctor died several years ago, and Joe converted the former waiting room and examinations room into a den. There is a pool table in the den, naturally, and it is the one that Balsis won his World Championship on in New York. A dealer in Harrisburg, Pennsylvania called after the tournament and told Balsis that he had the table. Balsis was curious but skeptical. The table he had played on in New York had a cigarette burn on the rail that Balsis had caused by forgetting a cigarette during the tension. The cigarette burn was still there and Balsis bought the table. Since then, he's always wondered how many other champions have the table they won on.

There is little doubt that Balsis will win tournament after tournament. He had many years to think about pool, while cutting meat in Minersville. Now that he's back in the game, he has to make up lost time. There were Willie Mosconi's years on top, then Luther Lassiter's. It appears that the next few years will be Joe Balsis's. Or if not, someone with a fast stick will have a hard time taking them away from him.

# 10
## Ardell LaSieur – Spirit of St. Louis

Ardell "Blackie" LaSieur is caught in a quandary that most pool players would envy. He has the relative financial security of a growing billiards supply business and the day-to-day problems of a 12-table billiards room, but the two interests have left him little time for his own game and tournament appearances. But he does manage to get to the B.C.A. Opens and the Jansco's Johnston City tournament, just a few hours drive from St. Louis.

It isn't that he doesn't want to compete—he doesn't have the time.

"When tournaments are closer—I'll drive. But I can't take the time to go places like Las Vegas, for instance. Besides I like my businesses better. It's getting so I have to leave home."

His home is Florissant, Missouri, a St. Louis suburb and his businesses are the Grandview Billiards Supply Company and the Cue and Cushion Club.

"I quit the game ten to twelve years ago. At that time I was a one-pocket and nine-ball player. I played a good game of snooker, but I wasn't a straight player. There were several reasons why I left billiards. First, I was in an automobile accident. I received a broken pelvis, broken ribs, and other injuries. I was in the hospital for three months. I had also developed an ulcer. So I got out of the billiards business and quit playing."

Ardell LaSieur and wife Jewell, who also shoots pool. LaSieur got his nickname "Blackie" from Minnesota Fats.

Prior to the accident and the ulcer, LaSieur had operated the Delmar Recreation, a billiards room in St. Louis, now called the Uptown Recreation. He had run billiards rooms since he was 20 years old. And the combination of the accident and the ulcer soured his interest in his own game.

He left billiards for five years and worked for a lighting fixtures business.

After that five year haitus, he returned to billiards, first as the operator of the Cue and Cushion and, for the last three years, as the owner of the billiards supply business. He sells Brunswick and AMF tables. He was the first person west of the Mississippi to have a billiards house as part of a shopping center.

And although he says that he hasn't found his stroke after the five-year lay-off, his comeback in tournament play has been steady. In the B.C.A. Open in Chicago, LaSieur tied for ninth in straight and one-ball and was 17th in nine-ball and tied for 16th place overall. In the 1967 Jansco tournament in Johnston City, he was in the money in straight and nine-ball.

LaSieur got the nickname "Blackie" from the king of billiards nicknames, Rudolph "Minnesota Fats" Wanderone.

"It's been a long time ago," he says. "Fats and others gave me the nickname Blackie and it just stuck. Sometimes they used to call me Blackstone, but "Blackie" is what it is now.

"My wife and I will drive to tournaments if they are close—I come and just play for what I can, and it helps the billiard room business back home. I have a fine regular business. I have customers when no other billiard room has any and I like it that way. I just can't get away. I don't even like to drive to Johnston City, which is the closest tournament from St. Louis. Usually I don't even have time for sleep. We open at ten A.M. and run until eleven or twelve P.M., seven days a week. And we have an orderly business. I have never had to stop a fight. We'll let youngsters play at 16, but they have to have their parents permission. There are still some I turn away. The Florissant Valley Junior College is planning to hold billiards classes at the Cue and Cushion and that means four classes and nearly a hundred students."

LaSieur's wife Jewell plays too. Blackie taught her the game and taught her well enough for a third place win in the third Missouri State Women's Championship. They have a daughter Pat, now Mrs. Pat Brannan, and they have two grandchildren, Bobby and Kelly.

"I've never hustled," Blackie says, "I've never been out of St. Louis to hustle. I might have been a better billiards player if I had done some hustling, but I just never did."

His hustle has been in the business. If he says, like Wimpy Lassiter always does, that his game is falling apart, and that he's lost his concentration and his nerves are shot, it's part of the hypochondriac con that some have.

Don't believe it.

# 11

## Stanley Morycz – King of Coney Island

In the summer, Coney Island is a squalling mass of humanity—a million or more people on weekends, swimming, eating corn-on-the-cob and snowcones, drinking pop, dripping ice cream on the sidewalks, talking, shouting, running, riding the roller coaster and the dodge-'em cars and the ferris wheel, and milling around like lemmings on the edge of the sea.

The 19th century Russian novelist Maxim Gorki called Coney Island "the nearest thing to hell on earth," when he first saw it, and during the summers it is exactly that.

Even in the winter, Coney Island looks like an overage dowager queen who has seen better years, now cheap and tawdry. In the cold, the beaches are deserted, the hotdog stands closed and shuttered, and the only thing that remains open then is Stanley Morycz's billiard room, over the dodge-'em ride on the midway.

Even with the distractions of Coney Island, Morycz (pronounced Maurice) runs a good room. And he is currently the New York State champion.

"I won the New York State title in May of 1967 in Jacy's Billiard Academy in Flushing," he says. "I had a 5–0 record for first place. It was a double elimination tournament and Anifrio Lauri and Barry Greenberg were the favorites. Lauri lost early and went into the loser's bracket. I beat Greenberg in the second game 125–

Stanley Morycz shoots a difficult double bridge shot. Use of the bridges for shots like this is one of the abilities that a good money player or tournament winner must have.

62 and Greenberg, then in the loser's bracket, had to fight through that bracket to face me again. I didn't expect to get to the finals, but I did. Greenberg beat everyone in the loser's bracket and in the finals, he would

## Stanley Morycz — King of Coney Island

have had to beat me twice for the title. I just had to win one game. I beat him 125–79 and he was 5–2 for second place."

That tournament victory has been the highlight of Morycz's billiards career, which has been as obtruse as any. Now 37, Morycz was in a recon outfit during the Korean War, then held a variety of odd jobs before becoming a bartender in a bar and grill in the Bar Ridge section of New York, near Coney Island. Tending bar at night at the Tickle Toe Inn, Morycz had time during the day to wander into a 42-table room, where another New Yorker, Peter Judice, began teaching him the pomp and circumstances of the game. Eventually the Verrizano Narrows Bridge cut Judice's billiards room in half and Judice, who wanted to retire, sold all his equipment to Morycz.

Morycz took the tables and moved to the Eastern Parkway section for a year, then bought all new equipment and moved to Coney Island, where the patronage tends toward the raffish but the business is good.

Judice taught him to play in 1959 or so, and in 1960 he entered his first tournament, the Eastern States Handicap. That tournament is set up so some players have to shoot for 125 points and some for 100. Favored entrants were Judice, Frank McGowan, Greenberg, and Tony "Meatballs" Pizaro. Morycz won it.

He felt, however, that the victory was premature and the handicap system of the tournament helped. So he didn't enter another tournament until the 1963 New York City Metropolitan. "I was very bad," he says, "I placed tenth or so. But I get better with practice and in 1964 I was fourth in the same tournament."

Because of the growing business in Coney Island, Morycz didn't enter any tournament during 1965, but in 1966, he was third in the Metropolitan and fourth in the New York State tournament, which was won by Jimmy Cattrano, Jr.

Stanley Morycz outside his billiards room at Coney Island.

Also during 1966, he entered and won the Brooklyn Invitational, and the New York City Interborough.

In 1967, in addition to the first place finish in the New York State tournament, he was second in the New York Metropolitan.

Like other players who run billiards rooms, **Morycz**

has trouble traveling to some of the better tournaments away from New York.

He shot in the B.C.A. Open in St. Louis and came in 19th out of 50 and went to Johnston City, Illinois for the Jansco's circus in 1966. He lost two close matches: 125–121 to Luther Lassiter and 125–123 to Ralph Greenleaf. He eventually had a 3–4 record, not high enough for top money at Johnston City.

"I just can't get away," he says. "I run four leagues in the room and I also teach billiards to about 20 people. I just don't make enough to afford to travel to places like Las Vegas, for the tournament there, or Burbank, California. I like to play tournaments when I get a chance, but the money is over-rated and the back-room action, in places like Johnston City, is also over-rated. Everyone knows everyone else, and there isn't too much action unless someone makes a bad game. Then everyone jumps on him. You can't play the big guys, and to play the others, you have to give away weight. It just depends on who makes the best game."

Morycz is married, but his wife Eleanor doesn't take much interest in billiards.

"The first time that I took her to watch, when I was in a tournament, I missed a ball and she screamed. That was the first and last time she watched a tournament. And then she doesn't understand the game either. She thinks that when everyone is dressed in tuxedos, then they all *have* to be making a lot of money."

Morycz is a slight man, with a soft voice. His one outstanding feature, to which he looks askance, is a dagger tattoo on his left arm. "I had that done in the service —in a moment of weakness," he says.

The New York area is not one of the best areas of the country for billiards coverage. Two of the big papers —*The New York Times* and *The Daily News* will write an article about who won a squash game in Liverpool,

Stanley Morycz, Coney Island billiard room owner and New York State champion.

England, but when Lassiter plays Crane, they never mention it at all, Morycz claims.

"It's the money. Money builds up the game and the game attracts more money. And the newspapers and TV people don't cover any of the matches unless there is big money on the game. The TV networks will pay a half-million dollars to show a golf tournament. But they pay less than ten thousand dollars for a billiards tournament."

As we talked in Morycz's billiards room, the heavy thuds of the dodge-'em cars shook the floors. And every few minutes, the subway—Coney Island is the terminal for the BMT subway from Manhattan—pulled away from one-half block away.

"It's possible that the combination of the subway and the dodge-'em cars could shake a ball into a pocket. But it's rarely happened," he says.

Eventually Morycz would like to get out of the room in Coney Island and either become a touring tournament player or—he hopes—get an advisory job somewhere.

"All the hotels in the Catskills and in Florida advertise in the newspapers that they have a resident "Golf Pro" or a "Swimming Instructor." Why shouldn't there be a place for a billiards instructor? All the golf professionals teach golf on the side, between tournaments, for a local country club. It ought to be the same for billiards."

Morycz's best game so far is straight pool. He has had, while practicing in his room, 11 runs over 150. But, as he says, "it wasn't in competition—so it was nothing." He has also tried some three-cushion.

"I just put in a three-cushion table. I'm not very good but I'm getting better at it."

Morycz considers Lassiter, Crane, and Balsis the best in the business, but also acknowledges that there are some fine younger players. "Dallas West is the best younger player I have seen," he says. "Pete Margo shoots some good stick, but I haven't seen him. I understand that he's a high run player. And of course, in three-cushion, Jimmy Cattrano will be the world's champion in a few years."

Morycz does not consider himself a finished player. "I run a lot but lose. I leave too many open shots for my opponents—I have to learn not to do that.

Looking over the squallor of Coney Island, past the gigantic Nathan's hotdog stand, past the roller coaster, and the gypsy palm readers' booths and the shooting gallery and the ever-present dodge-'em cars, Morycz's last comment seemed entirely in keeping with Coney Island:

"What this country needs is a President who plays pool."

## 12

## *Sheila Bohm – Impatient for Stardom*

If there is one criteria in the world of billiards, it's this: serious title-holders and tournament winners must always be approaching retirement age. Willie Mosconi won the last of his 13 world titles and played around for a few months, then retired. Luther Lassiter has kicked around for years and years before becoming a serious title contender, and Irving "The Deacon" Crane is also in his 50s.

Even on the women's side, the adage seems to hold true: the woman most expected to win major tournaments is Dorothy Wise, a grandmother in her 50s from Half Moon Bay, California.

And the younger players, Ronnie Allen, Eddy Kelley, Pete Margo and the rest all fear the older players, or at least consider them all potentially dangerous in any given tournament.

The women too, all watch Dorothy Wise. She is the lioness of the billiard world—and her reign is supreme.

There are a few players who don't much care for the reputation of the older players—deserved or not.

And one of the women who cares least for the prowess of Mrs. Wise and the others is 21-year-old Sheila Bohm, a Rochester, Indiana housewife and four-time tournament winner.

"Mrs. Wise won the B.C.A. Open in 1967 and that's

Sheila Bohm, Rochester, Indiana housewife, is one of the better young woman players.

fine," Mrs. Bohm says, "she had only a few years left to shoot for the title. That's OK. But I think that this year things will be different. It's time that some of the younger women, San Lynn Merrick, Jackie Gorecki, or I should grab the title."

Underlying that statement is the assumption that Mrs.

Bohm has the right to the title as well as anyone. And indeed she has. After only four years at the tables, she has won four major tournaments and she came in third in the 1967 B.C.A. Open at St. Louis.

Sheila Bohm's prowess at the tables came about in a typical way—she first began playing prior to her marriage. She shot pool in Rochester, Indiana with Fred Bohm, then her fiancé, now her husband.

"When I first began playing, Fred could beat me," she says, with a grin. "Now I've shot him right out of the game. He doesn't play anymore. He never thought that I'd become as good as I am—for that matter, neither did I.

"On a bet, more or less as a joke, Fred entered my name in the 1967 Indiana State tournament. That was in April of 1967, and I won it. The scores weren't even close. I won by margins of 75–28, 75–32 and 75–48.

"Since that time I have managed to practice regularly, first in Rochester, Indiana. Then when the room closed there, I traveled three times a week to Winemac, Indiana, to play in the Red Carpet Recreation Center. That is really a fine room. The owner, Dale Fritz, has 12 tables and over 700 yards of red carpet."

In January of 1968, Mrs. Bohm entered Joe Farhat's Mid-West Open in Lansing, Michigan.

"Joe is really kind to me," she says. "He established the Mid-West Open because there was no Indiana state tournament that year and I had to win a state tournament to get to the B.C.A. Open. But as it turned out, he needn't have bothered with the Mid-West Open. I traveled to Peru, Illinois and won the Illinois State tournament to qualify for the B.C.A. prior to the Mid-West tournament that Joe established."

The Illinois state tournament was held in Don's Ball and Cue in Peru, and Sheila didn't have much competition. She won handily.

With the two major tournament wins—the Indiana

State title and the Illinois title—she traveled to Farhat's Mid-West tournament and won that too, again without much trouble. In those three tournaments, she never lost a match.

Her latest tournament victory was again at Farhat's Velvet Rail, in the women's Capital City Open. She lost the first match to Geraldine Titcomb, by one point, 75–74, and had to climb through the loser's bracket. She did, successfully, and defeated Miss Titcomb twice in the finals for the title. The spectre of the early loss haunted Sheila and she beat Miss Titcomb 75–47 and 75–53.

The tournament that she remembers most vividly and yet gives her the most displeasure is the 1967 B.C.A. Open. There she easily beat all women relatively her own age—Jackie Gorecki, the Michigan State women's champion, Jeanne Ann Williams, and some others. But she was beaten, in turn, by two women Sheila considers over-age—Dorothy Wise and San Lynn Merrick. Back to back losses to Wise and Merrick knocked her out of the tournament, but her victories were enough for third place.

But that's not high enough: "The first two top winners of the year before don't have to win a state tournament. That's why I had to win the Illinois State title, or the Farhat tournament. I had to qualify for the B.C.A. Open. I intend to place first or second this year so I won't have to go to the trouble of qualifying for the next Open."

But Sheila changed her mind about the smaller state tournaments when she discovered that a few more wins in those tournaments would qualify her for the annual $1,000. Ewald Fisher Co. prize for the top woman money-winner.

Hope never springs more eternal than in the mind of a pool player; Sheila's ideas of winning the 1968 B.C.A. Open were not achieved and again the first place winner was Mrs. Wise.

Sheila beat her first opponent, Pamela Pritchard 75-16, but lost her next match, against Mrs. Wise 75-34. Sheila then won her next two matches, beating Karen Christensen 75-46 and nine-year-old Jean Balukas 75-50. She then lost to Chris Miller of Maryland 75-73 to end her tournament matches. She did, however, win $150 for the high run out of the money—19 balls.

Her competitive edge in the tournaments is a result of an oft-practiced but seldom acknowledged strategy: gambling on local tables.

"I don't gamble real high—but I do gamble almost every time I play in Winemac, Indiana. I hustle the boys and some of the older men too—they still think that pool is a man's game and no woman should be able to play it well."

Occasionally Sheila will take her kid brother along, as he is a pretty fair shotmaker too. They will really cleanup.

"No one, absolutely no one would think that a woman and a punk 15-year-old kid could beat anyone. We do," she says.

Mrs. Bohm works in the Rochester Nursing Home as a nurses aide.

"The nursing home is owned by my father-in-law and my Mother runs it," she says. "That's an ideal situation for taking time off and going to the tournaments. Without a job like that, I couldn't possibly make the tournaments, in Michigan and Illinois and the B.C.A. Opens."

Her gambling on the local Indiana tables makes her some money: "I usually don't win much—maybe $15 or so at quarter-a-game pool. But the winnings from the tournaments have helped buy our Firebird."

The Bohms' new Pontiac, bought partially with Sheila's tournament winnings carries a brass dash plaque, suitably inscribed: "This car made especially for Fred and Sheila Bohm."

"I'm a nine-ball player," she says. "I hardly ever play

Sheila Bohm.

straights, except for practice right before a tournament. I do play some eight-ball too, but never any snooker. And I guess I'm unusual for a woman—I like to play the rails. I'm known as a good bank-shot artist. I'd rather play banks than anything—it keeps the cue ball safe."

The Bohms live in an elegantly-furnished house trailer on the outskirts of Rochester. The view out their windows reveals the ubiquitous Indiana cornfields, bare in the winter, with snow and wind sweeping across the flatlands, but chest-high in the summers, with rows and rows of growing corn. It rustles and sighs, music to the ears of farmers in the Indiana agricultural belt.

Sheila's trophies for the state and national tournaments are prominently displayed in the living room of the trailer—now called a "mobile home"—and they include three small trophies for the high runs in the national. Her highrun in a national has been 19, but in Indiana, just practicing, she had hit 55 before missing.

"I just can't get the big runs when I need them," she complains.

"I get along with almost all the women at the B.C.A.," Sheila says. "Dorothy Wise didn't say much between matches, because she was concentrating on winning. And San Lynn Merrick didn't say much either—she's a college speech professor, but the rest of the girls—Jackie Gorecki, and Jeanne Ann Williams and the rest were great!"

Sheila's natural talent at the green tables is part of her general abilities as an athlete.

"I have always been a tomboy," she says, somewhat with resignation. "I have always been good at all sports—they just come right to me."

She has several bowling trophies scattered among her billiards trophies. For years she bowled regularly with teams in the Rochester vicinity. And for five years before she began shooting pool she was a catcher for a girl's softball team, the "Sport-Spot" team. She has also won second place in the Indiana state badminton tournament.

"The one thing that I'd like is to be called a National Champion. That's it. And I'd like to do it and capture the B.C.A. women's division while I'm still young instead of doing it like Dorothy Wise, when she's in her 50s."

Although Sheila Bohm has plenty of time left—years and years of tournament play ahead of her—she wants that national championship *now*.

And within a year or so, she's quite likely to get it.

# 13

## Jimmy Cattrano, Jr. – The Legacy of Hoppe

In 1941 Jimmy Cattrano Jr. was three years old and just old enough to toddle around on his own, playing on the floor of his family's Flushing, New York home. When his father saw him on the floor, he brought home a set of billiard balls and a stick for his son, like professional football players who give their sons a football, at the same age. To the surprise of his father, Jimmy took the balls and the cuestick, dropped to his stomach on the floor and began shooting pool. He took three pairs of his father's shoes, turned them sideways and placed them at the relative distance of table pockets. With his stubby fingers and the cue that was longer than he was, Jimmy began to shoot the balls into the shoes, occasionally stopping to pry a ball out of the toe of a shoe.

He kept at it on the floor, until he was big enough to use a box to stand on and shoot on a table. Then the local newspaper headlines tell the story. Clearly here was a child prodigy at the game:

> Jim Cattrano, Jr., Only 5, Follows
> In Steps of Willie Hoppe On Billiard Trail
> —March 29, 1944
> Flushing Youth
> Seen 2nd Hoppe
> —1944

Jimmy Cattrano Jr., three-cushion expert.

Budding Hoppe, 5, Wins
Law's Grace for Dad
—1944, when Jimmy was arrested for being a minor and playing in his father's billiards room.
Boy Billiard
Wizard Wins
at YMCA

—1944

Seven-Year-Old Cue Wizard
Thrills Long Island Sportsmen
Eight-Year-Old Jimmy Cattrano
Billiard Champ, Makes Movie
—early 1940s, when Jimmy starred in a movie short, "Cue Tricks" with Ruth McGinnis and Irving Crane.

From that start at pocket billiards at three, Jimmy played regularly at pockets until he was 15. Then he met Willie Hoppe, who gave an exhibition in his father's room, Jacy's Billiard Academy, in Flushing. No one wanted to play three-cushion with the great Hoppe, so Jimmy volunteered.

It was a close game. For the first 27 innings or so, Jimmy had a lead of several points over Hoppe. Then Hoppe speeded up the game, left only safeties for Jimmy to play, and eventually won—but only by a few points.

Hoppe was so impressed with Jimmy's play at the time that he suggested to Jimmy that he "give three-cushion a chance for six months," figuring that it would take Jimmy only that time to learn the game well. The six-month trial period has lasted for many years now, for although Jimmy plays pocket billiards in tournaments, his real love is three-cushion. And he should soon be the next world's champion at that game.

Cattrano's enthusiasm for three-cushion is apparent. After all the years at the game, he still practices three-cushion three or four hours a day, every day except Saturday.

His tournament record has lengthened too, beginning with the championship of the Long Island pocket billiard tournament in 1953 and 1954. In 1958 Cattrano was first in the Long Island three-cushion competition. In 1963 he had a 4–7 record for 10th place in the World's championships, held that year at the Hotel Commodore in New York.

Jimmy Cattrano, Jr. — The Legacy of Hoppe   117

In 1965 he traveled to Burbank, California for the Burbank Invitational tournament. There he was 3-17 for 19th place, but the tournament was in pocket billiards instead of three-cushion.

Jimmy Cattrano, Jr. and his father, who brought him a set of pocket billiard balls and a cuestick when he was three years old.

In 1966 Cattrano won both the New York State pocket billiard championship and the New York City Metropolitan pocket billiard championship.

During 1967 he won the Eastern States Three-Cushion tournament and during 1968, he won the Great Lakes Open (three-cushion) in May and the New York State Three-Cushion championship, in June.

In the B.C.A. Open, held at East Lansing, Michigan, during October of 1968, Cattrano was the favorite to take the three-cushion title. He easily won his first four games with scores of 50–34, 50–16, 50–46, and one forfeit win. Then he played Larry "Boston Shorty" Johnson, one of the best all-around players and a leader in three-cushion. Cattrano lost 46–50. He won once more, beating Bud Harris 50–49, but again lost to Boston Shorty 40–50. Shorty won first place and Cattrano was second, with a 5–2 record. He took home $600 in prize money.

"There used to be a lot of three-cushion play in the past," Cattrano says. "But now there doesn't seem to be so much. I'd like to see three-cushion built-up—have more players and more three-cushion tournaments. There really hasn't been much three-cushion action in the last few years."

Three-cushion is not just the absence of pockets on the table. It is a totally different world that takes a different stroke, a different eye, and a better idea of the geometry of the table.

"If your stroke is heavy, play three-cushion," Cattrano advises. Although not in the Minnesota Fats scale, Cattrano is heavier than most players and heft is important in three-cushion.

"Good pocket players can play three-cushion well—usually—but three-cushion players can't necessarily play straight pool. You can always go from a light stroke in straight pool to a heavier stroke for three-cushion, but you may not be able to change from three-cushion to straight."

### Jimmy Cattrano, Jr. — The Legacy of Hoppe 119

Now Jimmy works for his father, who has owned Jacy's Billiard Academy for over 30 years—closer to 40. The name Jacy is a combination of *James A. C*attrano's, and the two-floor, 28-table room is a favorite of eastern players. Jimmy now lives in Bayside, near Flushing, with his wife Constance and their children Joseph, 15, who "plays a

Jimmy Cattrano, Jr., ready to shoot a three-cushion shot.

little bit of pool," according to Jimmy; Julia, 14; Don, 13; Dino, 11; and twins, Jamie and Jim-Jim, 3.

Unlike pocket billiards players, Cattrano is not particularily anxious to leave New York for tournaments.

"Johnston City?" he asks, "sure, I'll go—if the Jansco's have a three-cushion division." Since it is unlikely that the Jansco brothers would move the highrollers and midnight gamblers off a table and convert it to three-cushion, Cattrano stays away. Cattrano does no hustling either in New York or elsewhere, but he is a good money player, who wins when the occasion demands.

"The New York area *was* a good area for billiards—but it isn't quite as good as it once was. Willie Hoppe was from New York, and of course, Irving Crane is from Rochester. Arthur Rubin, who is now dead, was a good New York player and Abe Rosen, from here, was the former New York State champion."

Flushing, New York, is about a half-hour by subway from Manhattan, past the remains of the disastrous New York World's Fair and past Shea Stadium, the home of the New York Mets. But it is worth the subway hassle to get to Flushing to meet the Cattranos, father and son, and to play in their room.

Jimmy tends to be quiet and unassuming, but it is a real treat to talk to his father, James Cattrano. The elder Cattrano has owned the room in Flushing throughout the height of billiard interest in this country and he has known most of the famous players of past years.

But his obvious favorite is his son.

"Oh, Jimmy, Jimmy, Jimmy," he croons, getting out two bulging scrapbooks of newspaper clippings.

"Mr. Hoppe and Mr. Petersen (the late Charles Petersen) really liked Jimmy. Here," he says, turning the pages of the books, sifting back through the clippings and the years. "Here—all these letters in green ink are from Mr. Hoppe. He wrote to Jimmy all the time. And if you knew Mr. Hoppe, you'll know that he never did much writing."

Written with almost a feminine hand, were post cards and letters, Christmas cards and birthday cards for little boys. All to Jimmy when he was young, from Hoppe.

"Mr. Hoppe really liked Jimmy," Jimmy's father says, "here's a dollar that Mr. Hoppe gave Jimmy. And here's a summons to appear in court, because the police found Jimmy playing in Jacy's when he was too young. Here's another letter from Mr. Hoppe again, see the green ink? Oh. Mr. Hoppe really liked Jimmy.

"Here was Jimmy on a local television show in the early 1940s. There were no television tapes then—all the shows were live. And there weren't any half-hour shows either. They went on until they ended. When they were over, they were over," he said.

"Jimmy was in a movie with Ruth McGinnis and Irving Crane and I'll tell you something. Ruth McGinnis was tops. She could easily beat all the women in pool today."

Jimmy Cattrano Jr. holds the idea that the triumvirate of Lassiter, Balsis, and Crane are the best men in the business today. But he also thinks highly of others, notably the man who most recently beat him—Boston Shorty. The late Harold Worst was also very good in three-cushion, Cattrano says, as is Crane, which most don't realize.

Jimmy Caras and Cisero Murphy are also top-flight too, Cattrano says, but he added that he really hasn't played all the pocket billiards experts enough to be able to evaluate their speed. Three-cushion is three-cushion and pocket billiards are pocket billiards and there is a Berlin Wall of difference between them, he infers.

It is unlikely that the name Cattrano will ever be synonymous with three-cushion billiards like the name Hoppe was. There is just not the interest in billiards now as there was when Hoppe barnstormed around the country. But it is likely that very soon Jimmy Cattrano Jr. will win the World's Three-Cushion title. He is close to the best of the current breed at the game. And when he wins the world's title, few except his parents will know that once upon a time, many years ago, a baby began to shoot pool on his stomach on the carpet, with his father's shoes as pockets.

# 14

## *Verne Peterson –*
## *They Call Him "The Slide Rule"*

Throughout most of his adult life, Verne Peterson's interests have been billiards and engineering. In the past few months, however, he has concentrated on billiards and it is fortunate that he has done so.

For Peterson has spent almost two years building what he describes as "the world's finest billiard room." If that is somewhat grandiose, his Billiard Palace is, at the very least, one of the finest rooms on the west coast.

But how it got that way is a long story.

Peterson came originally from Rockford, Illinois, where he was a practical engineer. Rockford, according to Peterson is a "tool town," and Peterson learned his skills the hard way—without the benefit of a college education. In Rockford, Peterson spent most of his time in machine design, special engineering projects, packing equipment, tool design and development, and other aspects of engineering.

But Peterson couldn't, even with a full career of engineering, keep away from billiards. He picked up the game, as most of the better players do, when he was young and eventually, before moving west, owned the Cue Recreation in Beloit, Wisconsin.

Then he was in and out of billiards, in and out of engineering, in and out of the contracting business. It

Verne Peterson shooting in his billiards room, the Billiard Palace.

was a period that, as Peterson says, I "did anything that I could to make a living at."

In 1959, Peterson, somewhat tired of the Rockford area and certainly tired of the snows and slush of midwestern winters, moved to Garden Grove, California and then to Bellflower, a suburb of Los Angeles.

For three years, 1960–1963, he worked for the Aero neutronic (space) division of the Ford Motor Company, specializing in procurements and products for the Armed Forces space programs. It was the height of his engineering career, as far up the ladder as he could go without advanced college training.

But then Peterson again became tired of engineering, at least as a full-time job and began again to operate billiards rooms. First he had one in Redondo Beach, California, and then in Anaheim, the home of Disneyland.

Eventually, he settled in Bellflower and began planning The Billiard Palace. Peterson had, by that time, an advantage that most billiard room operators didn't have— he had the engineering abilities and experience to design and make his own tables and make repairs, saving expenses with his own computations.

Peterson's dream of the world's finest billiard room was not realized quickly. For eighteen months, while he wrestled with the problems of tables, financing, equipment and installation, the Peterson family was without grocery money. "Toward the end of those months, even beans looked good on the table," he says.

But he finally opened his room in April of 1968, and it is one of the most distinctive rooms in the country. The crowning touch, which Peterson designed and manufactured himself is the over-the-table lights. He purchased outdoor garden lights, disk-shaped, and then designed and cut holes in the rims and inserted automobile tail lights in red, blue, green, and yellow. This in itself was not without some travail, as he had to obtain a special permit to use the lights. The state of California limits the use of some types of lights to police use only, and Peterson had to certify that he was not out to break California traffic laws with his table lights. Finally the room, lights and all, opened and since then has attracted such eminent stars as Ronnie Allen, Joe Balsis, and others who play exhibitions against Peterson. The red, blue,

Verne Peterson standing in front of his billiards room, the Billiard Palace.

green, and yellow over the tables give the room a distinctive warm glow and were well worth the hassle, according to Peterson.

And because the west coast is known as the home of film stars and film work, Peterson has become the reigning consultant for various billiards shots for television and films.

He did trick shots for the Frank Sinatra-Dean Martin film, *Robin and The Seven Hoods*, during which he dressed in the principals' clothes and shot, as the cameras ground through their footage behind his back. After the day's shooting, he handed back the cue, picked up a check for $150, and Sinatra and Martin moved in for the close-ups.

He also did some work for the universally-panned film *Beach Blanket Bingo*, with Frankie Avalon and Annette Funicello. For that fiasco, Peterson had to draw an eight ball into someone's mouth. Just whose mouth it was, Peterson forgets, and it is probably just as well.

He has also worked for the *Mr. Ed* show, in which he created shots for Tommy Gomez and Alan Young.

Perhaps Peterson's most memorable work with the tinsel world of show biz was consultant work on the *Dean Martin* television show. For five weeks, Peterson gave weekly lessons to Dean Martin, so that Martin himself could accomplish the trick shots seen on the opening credits of the show.

"It was a big kick, working for Martin. I worked on the set one day a week, for about an hour and one-half, and got $100 per week. But it certainly was more interesting than some of the other jobs—I could watch more of the technicalities of putting the show together."

Peterson's record in the national tournaments is as creditable as his film and television work. In the BCA Open at Chicago, Peterson finished eighth. To enter that, he had to win a state tournament and did so by beating Jack Breit in the Arizona state matches—two games in a row.

He was then eligible for the next BCA in St. Louis, but passed up the opportunity because he was building the Billiard Palace at the time.

In the last BCA in Lansing, Michigan, Peterson finished 12th. He won his first three games against colorless opposition, then lost to Danny DiLiberto. Peterson was shooting excellent pool against "The Wonderful Wop," as DiLiberto is called, and had only 13 balls between him and the end of the game, but Peterson admits that he "lacks the killer instinct" present in some other players and he blew a shot. DiLiberto got up and won it. Peterson was then knocked out of the tournament by Cisero Murphy, by a margin of 65 balls.

Peterson has done well in several lesser tournaments. He won the Western States Open in 1965, tying Richie Florence, then beating him for the title. He has been in the money three times at the Stardust in Las Vegas and was fifth in straight pool and 12th in nine-ball in the Long Beach, California International.

Peterson plans to compete in the next Stardust, in Las Vegas, but admits that eastern tournaments—the Jansco's Johnston City, Illinois tournament and some of the others are a bit too far to travel, especially now that he has the Billiard Palace to watch. It is open from ten A.M. until two A.M. seven days a week.

Peterson also plans, in addition to regular play at the Palace, sales and service of tables and custom cues. He has begun training mechanics to service tables, and his operation is a two-floor affair. The billiard room is on the second floor and on the first floor, facing the main street of Bellflower, is an exhibition room and sales department. Peterson's skills at engineering have enabled him to begin making $60 custom cuesticks, which are comparable to any custom cue that you can buy, he says. Peterson has his own equipment for their manufacture.

Like Joe Balsis, Mosconi, and the late Charlie Petersen (no relation), Verne has served on the Brunswick staff, but in the last few years has not worked steadily for Brunswick. He does give exhibitions on his own, however.

The Peterson family now includes his wife Mary; a son Rodney, who lives in Rockford, Illinois; Gregg, 18, who helps at the billiard room; and two daughters, Gail, 15, and Debra, 13. Gail is in high school and Debra is in junior high.

Verne Peterson shoots in the foreground in his room, the Billiard Palace. The line of white dots above the tables are Peterson's custom-built lights.

Peterson would also like to have regular challenge matches at his room, thereby making it one of the few rooms to regularly feature the top players.

"In the next few months, I'll begin those matches and I think that there will be two rooms—mine and Weenie

Beenie Staton's on the east coast—which will have the better matches."

The Billiard Palace *is* one of the nicer rooms currently in operation, as this writer can attest. That Peterson has devoted considerable work to the room is obvious. That he is remarkably adept with the cuestick, is equally obvious.

At the age of 49, Verne Peterson now has what he likes best—a fine room, a planned exhibition and match schedule, a good beginning on a billiards sales and supply business, and the occasional jobs that take him into the tinsel and fakery of the Hollywood film set.

In the vernacular of the engineers, a slide rule is sometimes called a "slipstick." Verne Peterson, it must be concluded, is equally at home with a slipstick or a cuestick.

# 15

## Mary Canelos – Co-ed with a Hot Stick

Mary Canelos is five feet two inches tall, with sparkling eyes and brown hair. She has a very, very engaging smile but give her a cue stick and she's no longer little Shirley Temple gone to college. She's close to the best there is, and she'll beat you and walk away giggling.

In addition to her hot stick, Mary is one of the most interesting players in the game. She bubbles over with enthusiasm, and seems to TALK IN CAPITAL LETTERS for EMPHASIS. It's obvious after only a few seconds that that she has a tremendous time with billiards and college in general.

At Illinois, they call her "Mary The Pool Shark," or "The Hustler." She just missed the 1967 finals of the Association of College Unions Intercollegiate Billiards Tournaments by a fraction of a point. The four finalists were determined on a balls-per-inning basis and they had to practically use a slide rule to determine the winners. Mary missed the finals by one-one hundreth of a point.

"Gimme a break," she says about it and that's her favorite expression. She uses it constantly, with meanings ranging from "good grief!" to "rats!"—from happiness to utter disgust and anger.

"The Purdue sectionals weren't tough at all, except for the final game," she says. "I was scared during the final match because the girl was from Purdue and all the crowd was from Purdue and there was no one I knew.

Mary Canelos, third-ranked co-ed in the nation.

## Mary Canelos — Co-ed with a Hot Stick

The advisor from Illinois said 'Don't worry, it's no big thing!" BUT IT WAS. I have a clutch factor of 99 percent in front of ONE MILLION people. GIMME A BREAK!"

But 1968 was different. She was determined to get to the finals and the year of practice helped. She made it; she was ranked number four going into the National Intercollegiate Tournament, held at the University of West Virginia, in Morgantown during the last week-end in April.

Mary came through the tournament with the third place trophy. She beat Dorinda Perrin of the University of Maine 35–34, was defeated by Donna Reis of the Univer-

Mary Canelos bridges for a difficult shot.

sity of Missouri 35–22, and lost a close match to Gail Allums 35–33. But she still has two years of college to complete.

"I play 14.1 mostly. I began in July of 1967, at a room in Chicago—home—and now I play every day. Usually from 2 until 5 P.M. or from 2 until 8 P.M. Eating dinner is a waste—I'm too busy doing something else to eat. Sometimes if I'm busy with classes I miss a day, but usually I shoot every day."

On the rare days Mary misses getting to the Illinois Union tables because of her classes in art. She's a sophomore in art and has been at it "for as long as I can remember." This year she has classes in Anatomy, Life Drawing, Painting, Art History, and Composition. Her Composition course interests her more than the rest because she's working on a huge—HUGE—wooden piece that bears vague resemblance to a nutcracker.

"It's on a sculpture scale and I call it my 'Headsmasher.' WOW! I was working it the other day and had to hold this arm up" . . . she explains with her hands . . . "and I had to hold it up and work on the bottom. When I turned POW! I slipped and the arm came down and hit me on the head. The instructor laughed. He said that I'd kill myself with that thing before I got it done."

"After it's done—then what?"

"I'll keep it in my dormitory room."

She's also working on another big piece she calls "Cross-Section of Sterility," which is even harder to explain.

"I want to do two things—I want to go back and teach art in high school. When I was in high school, we weren't taught ANYTHING. I was never directed or stimulated in high school. Boy, I want to help those kids, I want to teach 'em control."

Then she pauses.

"I want to be a bum painter. I want to live in places like Acapulco and Madrid. WOW!"

Mary Canelos — Co-ed with a Hot Stick 135

Mary Canelos and her "Headsmasher," a massive art project.

In more ways than just her billiards game, Mary is unique.

"I don't get along in the girl's dormitory," she says. "I'm not concerned. I don't like to gossip. All the girls there have to read their own copy of *Seventeen* magazine every month—and con guys into big dates on weekends. Like some of these girls are really broken up—REALLY TORN UP—if they don't go out on Friday nights."

She mimics: "My social life will be ruin-ed!"

Then she's serious: "I can't stand that."

Her clothes are different too. She usually dashes to the Illini Union to shoot pool between her art classes, dressed in her grubby art clothes—jeans and an old shirt. But occasionally she'll put on a mini-dress and shoot pool and "psych out" the guys.

"WOW! That's really fun. Here I am, a picture of innocence, creaming this guy. They're all used to my art clothes."

Most of her clothes "have to be wild."

"I never had liked frilly clothes. I'm more comfortable in slacks and sweatshirts. I used to make excuses—I hate pink and like dark colors and bell-bottom pants. WITH STRIPES. I love stripes. I have a pair that I call my 'Convict pants.' But for Christmas I was given some pink cloth and, well, I decided to make some dresses. So if I work at it, I can make a mini-dress in one day or so. Two days mebbe, with Bermudas under it so I can play in 'em."

Another of her big interests is music.

"I LOVE to do the Boogaloo," she says, giggling. "I dance every chance I get. I love music. There is no better way to have intercourse with music than to dance to it; sure you can listen, but to dance is to BE the music."

She ponders psychedelic music and musicians.

"The Rolling Stones. I LOVE the Stones. I'm really hot for 'em. I love sitar music and Ravi Shankar. I really dig some of the Beatles music. WOW! GIMME A BREAK!"

But even more than that, she likes billiards and likes beating guys.

"There used to be a guy here who thought he was the top stick. I beat him by 28 balls. WOW! He must have been terribly embarrassed. He just stopped coming in here (the Union). The last time I saw him he said "Pool doesn't mean anything to me, BUT IT DID. Some guys get so disgusted."

One of the biggest matches she has played was an exhibition with Jimmy Caras.

"Oh," she says, in indignation, "it was murder. He was big-hearted—he broke the rack for me. I really clutched up. I made one ball. ONE BALL. I was so scared. He ran 75. He said 'We better give this girl a break,' and tried an impossible two-rail shot and missed. Deliberately. I ran seven balls and missed."

She winked at the crowd. "Just thought I'd give you a break, Jimmy," she said then.

Her billiards constantly gets her into difficulties with guys at Illinois. "I was dating a guy here for a while. We used to go to shows and things like that. One night he said, 'Let's do something different, let's play pool.'

GIMME A BREAK!

"We went down to the Union and I pretended I never saw the place before. He had to show me how to hold the stick and how to bridge. I was missing a lot when one of the officials came up. 'What do you want on this billiards trophy?' he asked. Wow! My date said 'Let's quit fooling around, shall we?'

"I beat him bad—really bad—and I never saw him again."

Her parents, Mr. and Mrs. Constatine Canelos are "pretty liberal," she says. "They know that the rooms are 'billiard parlors' now instead of 'pool halls.' They have given me a curfew of midnight, but my playing is OK.

"I love to play in Bensinger's in Chicago. What atmosphere. WOW!" she says and her eyes light up. "I've seen some really savage games in there—nine-ball especially."

One of the billiard parlors in Chicago lets her play for nothing. She beats all the guys who want to play and the management gets its money back from the guys who practice and practice so they can "get her" later.

But billiards and dancing and dates don't interfere all that much with her classes. In her first year at Illinois, she got a 3.7 and a 3.9. An 'A' average is 4.0. This semester she'll have a 3.9 or a 4.0, she says.

"I've been doin' a lot of bookin' (studying), especially in Art History.

"Next year I'll begin to finish up in these sequences. Take more Art History, more painting and like that. I might take a literature course or something. My minor is Speech. Because I TALK a lot," she giggles.

"But I love art here. They really have some fine people."

But she doesn't plan any deviation from her game. "I have to watch my 'image' in the Union and that's a drag. But I'm a shotmaker and my game gets better.

"After all, position is the name of the game, isn't it?" she asks coyly.

## 16

## *Gail Allums –
Iowa's Number One Double Threat*

If Gail Allums beats you in billiards, don't offer to bowl with her—she might beat you again. For Gail, a University of Iowa co-ed, is a natural champion in both sports and has the rankings to prove it.

"I never played pool before coming to the University of Iowa. I played in the Memorial Union on a date. Now this is the only place I shoot," Gail says.

That casual date as a freshman introduced Gail to a sport she had never seen. She found that she had a good eye, a good stroke, and a keen appreciation for the game.

After that first date, Gail began to practice alone in the Union Recreation center between classes. She is a physical education major at the University. Last year, with the help and encouragement of Robert Froeschle, manager of the Iowa Union bowling and billiards area and manager of the B.C.A. tournaments, Gail entered the women's division of the Intercollegiate Billiards tournament. She also entered the bowling section of the Intercollegiate Tournament at the same time.

Gail breezed through a 12-school competition held at the University of Iowa in February, 1967, and was entitled to compete in the regionals of the billiards tournament, held at the Union of the University of Minnesota campus.

The Lions and the Lambs 140

Gail Allums, the best co-ed billiards player in the nation.

She was naturally concerned about the competition in billiards and bowling at the same time, but Froeschle told her to concentrate on the bowling, and worry later about her billiards game.

She bowled nine games, had a 209 game, a 546 series and kept her usual average of 150.

"She was about number three girl in all events in the bowling regional," Froeschle said. "Iowas came in second as a team. We were beaten by three points by a team from Mankato State College in Minnesota."

And although that ended Gail's bowling, she made it

Gail Allums, University of Iowa co-ed.

through the regional billiards elimination and into the nationals, held at Oregon State University, Corvallis, Oregon, April 20-22, 1967. She was ranked third going into the nationals, based on a balls per inning average. Her closest game in the national was a 35-14 win. The Oregon tournament was based on short, 35-ball games for girls and, as Gail said, "The girl who started out usually won."

Gail placed third. Shirley Glicens of the University of Miami, Florida was first and Catherine Stephens of Western State College, Bellingham, Washington was second.

"It was smooth sailing until Oregon, then I panicked," Gail laughs. She didn't panic much. It was a close tournament—the last place finisher beat the first place winner and the field was closely bunched.

"That trip to Oregon—everything—was paid for by the University of Iowa. I'll go anytime for that."

When she returned to Iowa, television station WHO in Des Moines asked her to round up a bowling team. Gail and the other girls on the University team played a team from Iowa State University on the show, "Let's Go Bowling."

And go bowling she has.

"My mother, Earleen, and my father, Theodore, are in bowling leagues in Maple Park—a suburb of Chicago. I always went along and it was a matter of me finding a league to play in." She has been bowling for about ten years. Recently she turned 22.

Gail works for the Poverty Program in Chicago during summers away from the University of Iowa. She practiced at home and prepared for the next intercollegiate billiards tournament. "I got a lot of practice during the summer. In school, I only practice once a week or so for about an hour."

The year of practice helped Gail's game. Froeschle also helped here with tips on position game and stroke. The next time, she did not attempt to bowl and shoot billiards at the same time, and the results paid off. She quickly and easily won the regional billiards tournament and ended up the number one finalist, going into the nationals, held at the University of West Virginia, in late April, 1968.

At the 1968 intercollegiate tournament, Gail's stroke and eye were deadly. She won two easy matches, beating Donna Ries of the University of Missouri 35–13, and the same day beat Dorinda Perrin 35–15. Her toughest match was against Mary Canelos, who was her room-

## Gail Allums — Iowa's Number One Double Threat

mate at the tournament. Gail won that match 35–33, and won a trophy that stands nearly waist-high. Jimmy Caras gave it to her, and he was the pro at the tournament the year earlier who gave her the third place finish trophy that year.

Even with the flu, Gail won easily. In her match with Donna Ries, Gail lost the lag and had to break. But Miss Ries missed her first shot, Gail ran 14 balls. Again Donna missed and Gail ran another ten.

The day after Gail's tournament victories, she entered a Chicago hospital for an operation and a lengthy convalescence. Her case of the flu was actually an undiagnosed gallstone attack. And her health insurance expired several days before the tournament began.

Back at the University of Iowa, signs began appearing on the walls of the Union billiards area. FRIENDS OF GAIL, they read, HELP HER GET OUT OF THE HOSPITAL. A cigar box was placed on the desk for contributions to help pay her hospital expenses.

"It was really fantastic," said Bob Froeschle, "even sick as she was, she was making shots out of the middle of the rack that the other girls didn't even see."

"Billiards was a challenge to me at first and I was determined to get better. Now my friends call me 'The Hustler,' " Gail said.

"She is very well co-ordinated and has as fine an eye for the game as anyone I've seen in the last few years," Froeschle said.

Gail's steady date at Iowa is Huston Breedlove, a regular on the University of Iowa basketball team, "the Hawks." "I beat him at billiards and we'll shoot some baskets and I usually beat him at that too," Gail says, with fire in her eye. Huston is quite a bit taller than she is and billiards notwithstanding, he shoots a mighty mean basketball game.

"I don't like eight-ball—that's a luck game," Gail said.

She prefers straight pool, and she can regularly run 25–30 and up, when she's feeling right.

Gail has been the subject of in-depth articles in *Ebony* and *Sepia* magazines and she has had several articles done about her for *The Daily Iowan*, the morning University of Iowa newspaper. Just like the professionals, Gail is not afraid of any player, no matter what his reputation is. During the regional play-off, held at Iowa, Joe Balsis gave exhibitions and watched the college players. He was very impressed with Gail and gave her several useful tips about the game and how to play under tournament conditions. Balsis doesn't watch and advise just anyone who shoots a fast stick.

After graduation, Gail plans a career with the Poverty Program or a career in physical education. But in the spring, on a clear Iowa day, Gail discovered golf. It was just another game that she hadn't played, but she admits that it fascinates her. And, she says, she might just give up billiards and bowling for golf, at least during golf weather. Billiards' loss may be golfs' gain—but don't count on it. She likes the thin air of tournament caliber pool.

# 17

## *Robert Froeschle – Man in the Middle*

From a billiards standpoint, Robert Froeschle lives in the best of all possible worlds. The pros know him as the tournament director for the Billiards Congress of America (B.C.A.) Opens—in East Lansing, Chicago and St. Louis. But few of them know of his other billiard world—the collegiate scene.

Since 1955 Froeschle has been associated with college billiards as the manager of the recreation section of the University of Iowa Memorial Union. In 1957 he began work as tournament director of the Association of College Unions Intercollegiate Billiards tournament. In 1964 he became committee chairman for the organization.

But from a controversial standpoint, Froeschle is best known for his double-elimination scheduling for the BCA opens. "The problem here is one of logistics," he says. "At the BCA Opens tournaments, we have just so many tables and just a set number of hours to operate in. We have to work it all out to furnish morning, afternoon, and evening crowds with good matches and we have to keep the tournament short because most of the pros pay their own expenses.

"The double-elimination tournament is more difficult to establish and run than, for instance, the round-robin tournament that the Janscos operate in Las Vegas. It wouldn't work for us in the BCA Opens, because—if we had 48 players like we had in St. Louis—we'd have to schedule

Robert Froeschle in the Iowa Memorial Union, University of Iowa.

each of them for 47 matches. It just can't be done. We can't tie up a player for that long."

When a player loses a match in the double elimination schedule that Froeschle sets up, he is dropped into the losers bracket and must keep winning to stay in competition. If he loses a second match, he's out.

"The problem here is that once a man drops into the losers bracket, he must play back-to-back matches to stay in. At St. Louis, for example, Jimmy Caras, who won, had to play about eleven matches to win, while Luther Lassiter, who placed second, had to play only about six matches.

"Some of the professionals don't like the system, especially the younger ones who don't understand the problem. But Caras pointed out to them that the results are the same—all you have to do is just not lose, or just lose one match—and you're the champ."

It isn't as easy as it sounds. Froeschle spends at least 40 hours establishing the schedule. Then during the tournaments, he has to keep track of matches, referees, scorekeepers—everything. He has to keep it moving.

Froeschle also tried to let every player know when his first match is and when he'll shoot his subsequent matches. So far, Froeschle has not been forced to change a match. Some run late or short, but the times and tables have come out right.

The professionals aren't like the college kids. The college tournaments are easier. "First of all, there are fewer finalists to deal with. There are only four in each division. The schedule is set beforehand. There is no pressure of money—no $3,000 first prize—the kids merely have the glory of winning and taking the trophies back to their schools. "There is less worry, and" Froeschle pauses, "less time on your feet.

"The pros know all the technicalities—they know the ways to gain advantages—it's harder to keep ahead of 'em. But the college matches are usually well balanced and very good. One year—I think it was at New Mexico—we had an exhibition after the last match. The winner played Willie Mosconi, who was there to give an exhibition for the kids. The men's winner—I think he was from Indiana—gave Mosconi fits. The kid was shooting well until he made one mistake—just one—and Mosconi ran out on him. That's the difference between the kids and the pros—when you're playing the pros, you can't even make one mistake."

If Froeschle can't remember where exactly he saw certain matches it's certainly excusable. Since 1956, the collegiate tournaments have been held at Michigan State University, the University of Iowa, Iowa State University, Illinois, Indiana, Purdue, Kansas State, New Mexico, Arizona, Oregon State University, Minnesota, and Florida. Froeschle has seen them all.

"Part of the idea of the collegiate tournaments is to increase billiards interest in the area in which the tournament is played. At Iowa, we had a capacity audience—3,000—for every match. It's natural—we had the cream of the college billiards world.

"We also try to have a pro in to give exhibitions, too. For years Willis Mosconi came in. In the past, we've also had Joe Balsis. In the first year at Iowa, Willie Mosconi had a stroke and Brunswick sent Charlie Petersen. That was Petersen's last public appearance before the illness that eventually led to his death.

"It was through Charlie Petersen that the college tournaments got started. Prior to 1937, the tournaments were held by mail. The colleges would send in the results of their best matches and the winners would be named by mail. Petersen started the face-to-face competition."

The big difference between the professional and the collegiate tournaments—other than the fact that the pros know all the angles—is the length. The college tournaments are three-day round-robin finals with men's division, women's division, and three-cushion play. In the past there was a straight rail competition but it was abandoned because it was too boring.

Froeschle, a man on a tightrope in two worlds of billiards, has had plenty of experience. He began young. "My grandfather had a table in his basement. When I was ten or eleven he taught me how to play. My uncle ran a billiard parlor called the Clubhouse Cigar then. In those days I was able to meet touring pros like Willie Hoppe. I got a chance to hold a stick against them, certainly not play against them, but just meet them and shoot. That's what started everything. I worked for my uncle when I was in college and when I graduated from the University of Missouri I got into bowling and billiards as an assistant manager of some lanes in Bettendorf, Iowa.

"One of the touring pros who stopped at the University of Iowa, then went on to Bettendorf and told me that he had put my name in the hat for a job at the University of Iowa. I said 'thanks' and 'what's involved there?' They wanted someone with a college degree and some experience to manage their bowling and billiards operations at the Union. I began in Iowa City in 1955.

"We (at Iowa) are on an equal basis with any school, in our program and certainly in our facilities. We're more fortunate than some other schools, we don't have the communications problems others have. We're able to work with the college students personally and because Iowa City has minimal outside activity, we're able to help the players."

As Froeschle implies, Iowa City is one of those fabled mid-western small towns that close when the sun goes down. Froeschle's bowling and billiards area not only supports itself financially, but also helps the rest of the Union. The area recently was renovated with new black and gold wall-to-wall carpeting (black and gold are the University colors). New paint on the walls, new house sticks, and table surfaces rounded out the face-lifting. The kids like the area—they come in droves.

"Recently we've been taking a count of the paying

customers. We have 300 a day—at least—and more during the weekends and nights. We're booked up solid."

The rate is standard, $1 an hour, and the profits pay for the rest of the Union areas—the Music Room, the crafts center, and other areas of the Union that can't support themselves.

Froeschle's main concern isn't the money but the kids. "We don't make the player—that's a natural talent—but we do help him with his stroke and his eye." And when Froeschle talks of helping, it's evident that he likes his work. The kids like him and respond to him. Billiards isn't just a vocation with Bob Froeschle, it's an avocation. He has a table at home. "I don't play regularly but I do play. I like it. It's a great game."

That "I don't play regularly" routine may be hustle he learned from the pros. Froeschle is better than he'll admit. But pool isn't his whole life. His family includes Jim, a senior and mathematics major at the University of Iowa (Jim has a 3.98 out of a perfect 4.00 'A' average), and Jeff, a freshman at Oregon State University. "He's at Oregon because he likes the skiing and because he's interested in forestry," Froeschle says. His daughter Judith is now married to a University of Iowa graduate and is now Mrs. Judith Goeche of Des Moines. "I'm a grey-haired old grandpa," Froeschle laughs. He and his wife, Marjorie, attend all the sports events they can at Iowa.

"She's with me all the way—we go to the football games, basketball, track, hockey, gymnastics, and wrestling. There just isn't a sport that I don't like." But more than anything else, he likes the professional game of billiards. You can tell when he talks about the pros.

"I'm very impressed with them. They're gentlemen, talented and sociable. You wouldn't know they are pros if you met them on the street. It's just that they have way up too," and Froeschle begins to rattle off names, one after the other, "Dallas West, a real comer, great control, Danny DiLiberto, Ed Kelly from Las Vegas, Lou "Shotgun" Butera, Steve Mizerak, Pete Margo . . ."

Sum total of Robert Froeschle, man of two worlds: a real gentleman, a sportsman, a pro.

# 18

## *The Hustler – The Renaissance of Pool*

In 1961 a small book that was largely ignored was made into a film that changed the world of pool overnight. The book was *The Hustler* by Walter Tevis and it was made into an extremely professional film of the same name directed by the late Robert Rossen and distributed by Twentieth-Century Fox.

It made super stars of two competent actors—Paul Newman and Jackie Gleason and it made a fortune for one hustler, Rudolph Wanderone, who previously had been moving back and forth under a variety of pool nicknames from New York Fats, to Chicago Fats, to Philadelphia Fats, to Baltimore Fats, depending on where he was at the time.

When the film came out he was instantly Minnesota Fats, after a character by that name in Tevis's book.

As Tevis says, "I researched the book by standing around in pool rooms in Louisville, Kentucky for five years or so. The actual writing took about one year, 1959, while I was attending the University of Kentucky at Louisville. Later I attended the University of Iowa and submitted the manuscript as my thesis project for a Master of Fine Arts degree.

"There were no changes in the manuscript when it was accepted for publication. The book did not sell terribly well as a hardcover book, but did sell extremely

Jackie Gleason starred in the 1961 film "The Hustler," with Paul Newman as "Fast Eddie." Gleason did his own shooting in the film. (Courtesy Pete McGovern, Jackie Gleason Studios)

well as a paperback and has gone through several printings."

Tevis's book captures the atmosphere of the pool world very well, although it must be stressed that it *is* a work of fiction and therefore exaggerates in some respects the real world of the pool player who shoots for money.

Technically it is a superb book. Tevis's descriptions of the matches between the fictional "Fast Eddie Felson" and the fictional "Minnesota Fats" are excellent:

> Someone flipped a half dollar. Eddie lost the toss and had to break the balls. He took the standard shot —two balls out from the rack and back again—three rails on the cue ball or the end cushion—and he froze the ball on the rail with only a bare edge of a corner ball sticking from behind the rack, to shoot at. Then Fats walked very slowly, ponderously, up to the front of the pool room, where there was a green metal locker. He opened this and took out a cue stick, one joined at the middle with a brass joint, like Eddie's. He picked a cube of chalk up from the front table and chalked his cue as he walked back. He did not even appear to look at the position of the balls on the table, but merely said, "Five ball, corner pocket," and took his position behind the cue ball to shoot.
>
> Eddie watched him closely. He stepped up to the table with short, quick little steps, stepping up to it sideways, bringing his cue into position as he did so, so that he was holding his cue standing sideways . . .
>
> And Fats' one victory did not affect Eddie, for Eddie was in a place now where he could not be affected, where he felt that nothing Fats could do could touch him. Not Eddie Felson, fast and loose—and, now, smart, critical, and rich. Eddie Felson, with the ball bearings in his elbow, with eyes for the green and the colored balls, for the shiny balls, the purple, orange, blue, and red, the stripes and solids, with geometrical rolls and falling, lovely spinning, with whiffs and clicks and tap-tap-taps, with scraping of chalk, and the fingers embracing the polished shaft, the fingers on the felt, the ever and always ready arena, the long, bright rectangle. The rectangle of lovely, mystical green, the color of money.
>
> And when Eddie had won a game and was lighting his cigarette Fats spoke out grimly, with words that

Eddie could feel in his stomach. "I'm quitting you, Fast Eddie, I can't beat you." *

Tevis acted as technical advisor to the film-making and Willie Mosconi was advisor for the shooting sequences. For several weeks prior to the actual shooting of the film, Mosconi spent hours teaching Paul Newman to hold the stick and shoot and act like a pool player. Mosconi was satisfied when Newman could shoot 20-25 balls on his own. Jackie Gleason, as Minnesota Fats, needed no such help. Gleason has his own table, and has known how to play since his early teens in Brooklyn. In fact, during his youth, before he became the nationally known television star, Gleason had hustled on his own for eating money in Brooklyn. So he was no stranger to the game and he was perfect for the role of "Minnesota Fats."

In the book, as in the film, "Fast Eddie" Felson, a young hustler, has plenty of ability but no character. During an early match with Minnesota Fats, Fast Eddie comes within a kiss shot, figuratively, of beating Fats, but is himself beaten by his own lack of "heart." A professional gambler, Bert, played in the film by George C. Scott, offers to guide Eddie to winning—for a percentage. A crippled alcoholic girl, Sarah, played by Piper Laurie, also helps Eddie when he is down, although neither he nor she realize it.

After the match with Fats, Eddie attempts to con a young kid and gets his thumbs broken for his trouble. With his thumbs broken, he is unable to shoot with the closed bridge and must bridge openly, across the flesh between his thumb and index finger. Eddie figures his speed is cut down about 20 percent. Eddie is taken by Bert to Louisville, during the racing of the Kentucky

---

* From pp. 36-37 *The Hustler* by Walter Tevis. Copyright 1959 by Walter Tevis. By permission of Harper & Row, Publishers.

Gleason has been a pool addict for most of his life and he shoots a good stick. He learned to play during his youth in New York and the role of Minnesota Fats in "The Hustler" was natural for him. (Courtesy Pete McGovern, Jackie Gleason Studios)

Derby, to meet a player named Findlay. Findlay almost beats him at three-cushion billiards—but not quite. Eddie has discovered something about himself—that inner something that separates a good player from a champion.

## The Hustler — The Renaissance of Pool

Eddie and Bert return to Chicago, and Eddie plays Minnesota Fats again. This time, after a marathon match, Eddie wins and is the uncrowned national king of hustling. Instantly he is the man to beat. Fast Eddie. The man who took Minnesota Fats. But Eddie discovers, to his chargin, that by winning, Bert automatically becomes his "manager" and if Eddie plays (and he has no choice) Bert automatically gets 35 percent. And there the book ends. In the film, there is the usual Hollywood happy ending: when Eddie discovers that he's been hustled into a bad deal with Bert, he walks out of the hall, leaving his championship for Fats to pick up again and leaving high action pool forever.

Theater or television showings of the film (re-released after its original release in 1961) never fail to "hype the gate"—increasing billiard hall business as much as 300 and 400 percent for several months. Billiard hall proprietors have suggested that everyone connected with billiards should contribute to the cost of showing the film on national television each winter at Christmas time (an unlikely time for this essentially seamy plot). The film had made the world of billiards a popular form of recreation for teenagers and other followers of Gleason and Newman.

It even impressed pool hustlers. Professionally there are few flaws to the film, except a tendency to exaggerate the seamy side of the business. As one hustler has said, "there is nothing wrong with that film, except it shows the world of the pool hustler as it was in the 1930s or so . . ."

Paul Newman regards it as the finest film he has performed in and now, speciality shops, psychedelic shops offer poster-size photos of Newman and Gleason from the film. Countless college students have hung the posters on their dormitory walls, then walked downtown to shoot like "Fast Eddie."

# Glossary – An Abridged Lexicon of the Game

ACTION—betting on games. "Fast action" is heavy betting.

A 'G'—one thousand dollars.

ANGLED—when the lip of a pocket prevents a straight shot from the cue to an object ball.

ARMY—betting money: "I've got my Army with me . . ."

BACKER—banker for a gambler. A non-player usually, who supplies betting money. The backer will usually cover all losses, but will take a percentage of the hustler's winnings.

BANK SHOT—a shot against a cushion and then into a pocket.

BILLIARDS—(or three-cushion billiards)—a game played on a table without pockets. Billiards is played with three balls, two white and one red. Each player (only two can play at one time) uses a white ball as a cue, and shoots to strike the other two. The cue ball must touch the cushions at least three times before striking the second of the two object balls. Billiards is a very difficult game, which demands a thorough knowledge of table angles and English. Billiards is played for money much less frequently than pocket pool.

BREAK—the shot that opens the rack; the first shot of a game.

BRIDGE—the act of holding the table end of the cue stick between the index finger and the thumb. There

## Glossary — An Abridged Lexicon of the Game

are two kinds of bridges: the closed bridge, with the index finger circling the cue, or the open bridge, with the cue sliding down the fleshy part of the hand, between the thumb and index finger. The closed bridge is more accurate and preferred.

Bridge also refers to the mechanical bridge, a device used to aid the player in making shots he couldn't normally make.

'C' NOTE—one hundred dollar bill.

CALL SHOT—a shot that requires the player to tell others which ball he intends to shoot into which pocket.

CAROM—a rebounding shot of one or more balls.

CHALK—dry lubricant for the cue tip. Without frequent chalking, scratches, or missed shots, are likely.

COMBINATION SHOT—a shot in which the cue ball strikes one or more balls. The object ball finally is hit by one of the other balls. A "chain reaction" type of shot.

CON—the art of making a bet, i.e., "to con." From the criminal's Lexicon—"the con game."

CUE BALL—the plain white ball that is hit into the numbered balls.

CUE STICK—the instrument of the game. Sticks usually weigh between 15 to 21 ounces and average 55 inches long. Pros and hustlers prefer a heavier cue, usually 20–21 ounces.

CUE TIP—leather end-piece of the stick, which is chalked.

CUSHION—the cloth—edge of the table rails.

CUT—to hit an object ball so it will angle.

DRAW or REVERSE ENGLISH—stroking the cue ball below its center will cause it to "draw" back toward the player.

DUMPING—a game a hustler deliberately loses to fool spectators who have bets on the match. Not a common practice. No hustler wants a reputation as a "dumper."

ENGLISH—the art of adding spin to the cue ball to

make it swing to the left or right after hitting the object ball. An essential part of a position game.

EIGHT-BALL—mostly an amateur's game. Players pocket either the low balls (numbered 1-7) or the high balls (numbered 9-15), the call the shot on the eight ball to win.

FOLLOW SHOT—stroking the ball above its center will cause it to follow the object ball. Follow shots are also used in position games.

FUN PLAYERS—lambs. Tournament winners. Amateurs.

HEART—courage. "He has real heart."

HIGH RUN—the number of balls consecutively pocketed before missing, in one game or tournament.

HUGGING THE RAIL—stroking action that will cause the cue ball or the object ball to roll down the rail along the edge of the table.

HUSTLER—a lion. A money player. Not an amateur.

JAW—when the object ball hits the sides of the pocket and bounces back and forth without dropping, it is said to have "jawed."

KNIFE AND FORK—hustlers' eating and sleeping money, i.e., "I have to remember my knife and fork" (remember not to bet it on a game and thereby risk going broke without money to eat on).

KISS—see carom.

LAMB—an innocent, an amateur.

LEMONING—winning in an amateurish fashion or deliberately losing a game.

LION—a hustler.

LOCK-UP—a game that can't be lost, because of inferior opponents. A cinch.

LOCKSMITHS—hustlers who specialize in playing lock-up games.

MAKING A GAME—setting up some action or betting.

MASSÉ—extreme english on the cue ball. Perhaps the

## Glossary — An Abridged Lexicon of the Game    161

most difficult shot in the game. The cue stick must be held almost straight up and down.

MIS-CUE—the scratch or miss shot, caused by inaccurately stroking the cue ball.

NATURAL—a simple shot; a lock-up shot.

NINE-BALL—a hustler's game, because it is fast and because bets can be made on individual balls, usually the five ball and the nine ball. Only the first nine balls are racked. They are pocketed in rotation (1–9) and the game is won by pocketing the nine. The nine can be pocketed on a good break shot or by shooting it from another ball, i.e., cue ball to three ball to nine ball to pocket.

ONE-POCKET—another hustler's game. Each player shoots into one corner pocket of the table.

O.P.M.—Other People's Money, which hustlers prefer to play with.

POSITION—the arrangement of the balls on the table. A good player can keep all balls in one-half of the table, thereby enabling him to shoot short shots and stay alive in the game.

RACK—the triangular arrangement of balls on the table before the game begins. Also refers to the wooden wedge used to form the balls into this shape prior to the game.

ROTATION—shooting the balls according to numerical sequence.

RUN—consecutively pocketing as many balls as possible. (See: high run.)

SAFE—to shoot so as not to leave your opponent room to shoot. "Playing it safe."

SCRATCH—a playing error in which the cue ball falls into a pocket. Some hustlers scratch deliberately to fake incompetence.

SETUP—an easy shot. See: natural.

SHORTSTOP—a player who can be beaten only by the top players.

SNOOKERED—a bad position, i.e., one in which the player can not shoot a straight shot.

SPEED or TRUE SPEED—the player's ability.

SPOT—to give away points or ball to ones opponent, i.e., to handicap.

STALLING—occasionally losing a game to keep an opponent betting.

STROKE—the act of hitting the cue ball. "To find my stroke," i.e., to develop a good swing. The stroke is as important as the golfer's swing.

SUCKER—the object of the hustler's attention, a loser.

TAKEDOWN—the amount of money won on the tables.

WEIGHT—points or ability. To "give away weight," is to give away points in a handicap game. "A heavyweight," is a top-flight player.

# Appendix – Standings
# Who Earns How Much

The five major billiards tournaments in the country are: the Stardust Open, in Las Vegas; the World's Straight Pool Championships, in New York City; the All-Around Pocket Billiard Tournament in Johnston City, Illinois; the National Championships, sponsored by the Billiard Congress of America and the Long Beach, California Open.

Here is how the top players divided the prize money: (1967).

## The Lions and the Lambs 164

| PLAYER | HOME TOWN | TOURNM. NO. | 14.1 | 9 Ball | 1-Pocket | Sanction Money | Total Earnings |
|---|---|---|---|---|---|---|---|
| Luther Lassiter | Elizabeth City, N.J. | 4 | $ 7,550 | $ 2,450 | $ 300 | $ 7,550 | $ 10,300 |
| Eddie Taylor | Suitland, Maryland | 4 | 1,300 | 5,100 | 2,500 | 1,800 | 8,900 |
| Joe Balsis | Minersville, Pa. | 3 | 4,200 | 1,800 | | 4,800 | 6,000 |
| Irving Crane | Rochester, N.Y. | 3 | 4,400 | 400 | 550 | 2,300 | 5,350 |
| Jack Breit | Houston, Tex. | 5 | 3,150 | 300 | 1,650 | 4,000 | 5,100 |
| Ed Kelly | Las Vegas, Nev. | 4 | 2,050 | 600 | 2,450 | 5,100 | 4,100 |
| Danny Jones | Columbus, Ohio | 3 | 1,250 | 2,300 | 550 | 500 | 3,600 |
| Cisero Murphy | Brooklyn, N.Y. | 5 | 1,200 | 1,400 | 1,000 | 1,000 | 3,350 |
| Johnny Ervolino | Brooklyn, N.Y. | 4 | 1,700 | 450 | 1,200 | 1,400 | 3,200 |
| Larry Johnson | Boston, Mass. | 2 | 400 | 750 | 2,050 | | 3,100 |
| Ronnie Allen | Burbank, Calif. | 3 | 650 | 1,450 | 1,000 | 1,350 | 3,000 |
| Jimmy Caras | Springfield, Pa. | 1 | 3,000 | | | 3,000 | 2,500 |
| Frank McGowen | New York, N.Y. | 4 | 2,000 | 400 | 100 | 1,900 | 2,050 |
| Mike Eufemia | Long Island, N.Y. | 2 | 2,450 | | | 100 | 2,050 |
| Dallas West | Rockford, Ill. | 2 | 2,050 | | | 1,450 | 2,050 |
| Danny Gartner | Clifton, New Jersey | 3 | 950 | 400 | 700 | 1,800 | 1,900 |
| Tom Halliday | Stanton Island, N.Y. | 1 | | 700 | 1,200 | | 1,750 |
| Danny DiLiberto | Miami, Fla. | 4 | 750 | 700 | 300 | 550 | 1,600 |
| Richie Florence | Torrance, Calif. | 2 | 1,050 | 100 | 450 | 1,250 | 1,550 |
| Billy Burge | Detroit, Michigan | 2 | 50 | 1,350 | 150 | | 1,550 |
| U. J. Puckett | Dayton, Tenn. | 4 | 500 | 150 | 900 | 250 | |

## Appendix — Standings Who Earns How Much

| PLAYER | HOME TOWN | TOURNM. NO. | 14.1 | 9 Ball | 1-Pocket | Sanction Money | Total Earnings |
|---|---|---|---|---|---|---|---|
| Marv. Henderson | Los Angeles, Cal. | 2 | 300 | 400 | 700 | 100 | 1,400 |
| Lou Butera | West Pittston, Pa. | 2 | 1,150 | | | 1,150 | 1,150 |
| Don Watson | Seattle, Wash. | 1 | | 1,000 | 150 | 1,150 | 1,150 |
| Jimmy Moore | Albuquerque, New Mex. | 2 | 150 | 600 | 300 | 600 | 1,050 |
| Joey Spaeth | Cincinnati, Ohio | 2 | | 300 | 600 | | 900 |
| Larry Perkins | Las Vegas, Nev. | 2 | 700 | | 150 | | 850 |
| Vern Peterson | Garden Grove, Cal. | 2 | 650 | 150 | | 600 | 800 |
| Richie Ambrose | New York, N.Y. | 2 | 200 | 600 | | 700 | 800 |
| Joe Russo | Trenton, N.J. | 1 | | 500 | 250 | | 750 |
| Louis Goff | Tampa, Fla. | 2 | 50 | 550 | 150 | | 750 |
| Art Cranfield | Syracuse, New York | 1 | 600 | | | 600 | 600 |
| Steve Mizerak | Metchen, New Jersey | 1 | 600 | | | 600 | 600 |
| Ardell LeSieur | Florissant, Mo. | 2 | 250 | 300 | 50 | 100 | 600 |
| Sam Blumenthal | Miami, Fla. | 1 | | 600 | | | 600 |
| Nick Vacchiono | Philadelphia, Pa. | 1 | | | 600 | | 600 |
| Onofrio Lauri | Seaford, N.Y. | 1 | 500 | | | 500 | 500 |
| Jim Relihan | Springfield, Mass. | 2 | 150 | 300 | 50 | | 500 |
| Alton Whitlow | Detroit, Mich. | 2 | 450 | | | 400 | 450 |
| Kazuo Fujema | Osaka, Japan | 1 | 400 | | | 400 | 400 |
| Al Gassner | Long Island City, N.Y. | 1 | 400 | | | 400 | 400 |
| Jack Colavita | Newark, N.J. | 1 | 400 | | | 400 | 400 |

The Lions and the Lambs

| PLAYER | HOME TOWN | TOURNM. NO. | 14.1 | 9 Ball | 1-Pocket | Sanction Money | Total Earnings |
|---|---|---|---|---|---|---|---|
| Bud Gromoos | Hicksville, N.Y. | 1 | 400 | | | 400 | 400 |
| Joe Diehl | Rockford, Ill. | 1 | 400 | | | | 400 |
| Tom Kollins | Wayne, Michigan | 2 | 350 | | | 300 | 350 |
| Marshall Carpenter | Tuscaloosa, Okla. | 1 | 350 | | | | 350 |
| Rags Woods | Los Angeles, Calif. | 1 | | | 300 | 300 | 300 |
| Maynard Parish | Monmouth, Ill. | 1 | 300 | | | 300 | 300 |
| T. J. Springer | Mantee, Mass. | 2 | 100 | 150 | 50 | 100 | 300 |
| Pete Margo | Union City, N.J. | 1 | 300 | | | | 300 |
| Billy Staton | Washington, D.C. | 3 | 250 | | | 100 | 250 |
| Rex Cannon | Las Vegas, Nev. | 1 | 250 | | | | 250 |
| Marcell Camp | Miami, Fla. | 1 | | | 250 | | 250 |
| Al Coslosky | Philadelphia, Pa. | 2 | 200 | | | 100 | 200 |
| Dan Tozer | Decatur, Ill. | 1 | 150 | 50 | | | 200 |
| Rodney Thompson | Kenosha, Wisc. | 1 | 50 | 150 | | | 200 |
| Tom Cosmo | New York, N.Y. | 2 | 150 | | 50 | | 200 |
| Steve Cook | Lima, Ohio | 2 | 100 | 50 | 50 | | 200 |
| Ronnie Atwell | Burbank, Cal. | 1 | 150 | | | 150 | 150 |
| Jack Perkins | Las Vegas, Nev. | 1 | | | 150 | 150 | 150 |
| Shirley Cloyd | London, Ky. | 1 | 150 | | | | 150 |
| John Hahn | DuQuoin, Ill. | 1 | | 150 | | | 150 |
| John Edwards | Bowling Green, Ky. | 1 | | 150 | | | 150 |

Appendix — Standings Who Earns How Much 167

| PLAYER | HOME TOWN | TOURNM. NO. | 14.1 | 9 Ball | 1-Pocket | Sanction Money | Total Earnings |
|---|---|---|---|---|---|---|---|
| Bryan Houser | Centralia, Ill. | 1 | | | 150 | | 150 |
| Marten Karmen | Denver, Colo. | 1 | | | 150 | | 150 |
| Red Baker | Hollywood, Cal. | 1 | 100 | | | 100 | 100 |
| Lew Bramlett | Columbus, Ohio | 1 | 100 | | | 100 | 100 |
| Joe Cosgrove | Atlanta, Ga. | 1 | | | 100 | 100 | 100 |
| Stanley Morycz | Brooklyn, N.Y. | 1 | 100 | | | 100 | 100 |
| Steve Carter | Washington, D.C. | 1 | | 100 | | 100 | 100 |
| A. Caramonica | Stratford, Conn. | 1 | 100 | | | 100 | 100 |
| Bob Noland | Aurora, Ill. | 1 | 100 | | | 100 | 100 |
| Charles Stone | Kenosha, Wisc. | 1 | 100 | | | 100 | 100 |
| LeMar King | Kansas City, Mo. | 1 | 100 | | | | 100 |
| Greg Stevens | Witchita, Kans. | 1 | 100 | | | | 100 |
| Sax Del Ponto | Redwood City, Cal. | 1 | 100 | | | | 100 |
| Frank Oliva | Chicago, Ill. | 1 | | 50 | | | 50 |
| Al Coslosky | Philadelphia, Pa. | 1 | | 50 | | | 50 |
| Jan Jansco | Johnston City, Ill. | 1 | | | 50 | | 50 |
| Pug Pearson | Las Vegas, Nev. | 1 | | | 50 | | 50 |
| *TOTAL MONIES WON* | | | $52,150 | $27,000 | $21,400 | $47,550 | $100,550 |